Job

Satan afflicts Job with painful sores, while Job's wife weeps at his feet. The story of Job addresses the question of how a benevolent God can allow suffering to exist.

Money at its Best: Millionaires of the Bible

Abraham and Sarah
Daniel
David
Esther
Jacob
Job

Joseph
Moses
Noah
Samson
Solomon
Wealth in Biblical Times

MONEY
at its
BEST

Job

Cameron Christine Davis

Mason Crest Publishers
Philadelphia

Produced by OTTN Publishing.
Cover design © 2009 TLC Graphics, www.TLCGraphics.com.

Mason Crest Publishers
370 Reed Road, Suite 302
Broomall PA 19008
www.masoncrest.com

Copyright © 2009 by Mason Crest Publishers. All rights reserved.
Printed and bound in the United States of America.

First printing

1 3 5 7 9 8 6 4 2

Library of Congress Cataloging-in-Publication Data

Davis, Cameron Christine.
  Job / by Cameron Christine Davis.
     p. cm. — (Millionaires of the Bible)
  Includes bibliographical references and index.
  ISBN 978-1-4222-0471-9 (alk. paper)
  ISBN 978-1-4222-0846-5 (pbk. : alk. paper)
  1. Job (Biblical figure)—Juvenile literature.
  2. Bible. O.T. Job—Criticism, interpretation, etc. I. Title.
  BS580.J5D38 2008
  223'.106—dc22
                                              2008020871

Publisher's Note: The Web sites listed in this book were active at the time of publication. The publisher is not responsible for Web sites that have changed their address or discontinued operation since the date of publication. The publisher reviews and updates the Web sites each time the book is reprinted.

Table of Contents

Job and His Wealth	6
Introduction: Wealth and Faith	7
1. Overview	11
2. Job's Life and Status	23
3. Much Is Tested	35
4. Mourning Song	43
5. False Comforters	56
6. The Hidden Face of God	76
7. Job in Literature	90
Notes	104
Glossary	110
Further Reading	112
Internet Resources	113
Index	115
Illustration Credits	119
About the Author	120

Job and His Wealth

- According to the Bible, Job was the wealthiest person of his time. "He had seven sons and three daughters, and he owned seven thousand sheep, three thousand camels, five hundred yoke of oxen and five hundred donkeys, and had a large number of servants. He was the greatest man among all the people of the East" (Job 1:2-3).

- Job was generous with his vast material possessions, sharing them with the poor and the sick, the orphans and the outcasts. According to Job 29, he never turned away travelers or beggars from his house without first feeding and clothing them.

- Job also had great spiritual wealth. The Bible says, "This man was blameless and upright; he feared God and shunned evil" (Job 1:1). Job thanked God daily for all His blessings and honored His laws; in return, God protected Job from harm.

- God allowed Satan to test Job's faith. Job suffered tremendously—his children were killed in a storm, his flocks were destroyed, and he was inflicted with painful sores. His friends mocked him and encouraged him to curse God for his misfortunes. In this sense, Job's is truly a riches-to-rags story.

- Job refused to curse God. Even at his lowest point, Job still possessed richness in faith. The Bible says that Job continued to worship God despite his misfortunes, saying, "The Lord gave and the Lord has taken away; may the name of the Lord be praised" (Job 1:20-21).

- Although God blessed Job, Job was also human and showed pride in all that he had done with his wealth prior to his downfall. God admonished Job, who promptly said "I despise myself and repent in dust and ashes." (Job 42:6)

- Because Job humbled himself before God and repented, the Bible says that God blessed him even more than before Job was cursed. Job had 10 more children, and his flocks were double their initial size (Job 42:12). Job was wealthy both in faith and in earthly possessions.

Introduction: Wealth and Faith

Many people believe strongly that great personal wealth is incompatible with deep religious belief—that like oil and water, the two cannot be mixed. Christians, in particular, often feel this way, recollecting Jesus Christ's own teachings on wealth. "Do not store up for yourselves treasures on earth, where moth and rust destroy, and where thieves break in and steal," Jesus cautions during the Sermon on the Mount (Matthew 6:19). In Luke 18:25, he declares, "It is easier for a camel to go through the eye of a needle than for a rich man to enter the kingdom of God"—a sentiment repeated elsewhere in the Gospels.

Yet in Judeo-Christian culture there is a long-standing tradition of material wealth as the manifestation of God's blessing. This tradition is amply reflected in the books of the Hebrew Bible (or as Christians know them, the Old Testament). Genesis 13:2 says that the patriarch Abram (Abraham) "had become very wealthy in livestock and in silver and gold"; the Bible makes it clear that this prosperity is a gift from God. Other figures whose lives are chronicled in

Genesis—including Isaac, Jacob, Joseph, Noah, and Job—are described as both wealthy and righteous. The book of Deuteronomy expresses God's promise of prosperity for those who obey his commandments:

> If you fully obey the Lord your God and carefully follow all his commands I give you today, the Lord your God will set you high above all the nations on earth. . . . The Lord will grant you abundant prosperity—in the fruit of your womb, the young of your livestock and the crops of your ground—in the land he swore to your forefathers to give you. (Deuteronomy 28:1, 11)

A key requirement for this prosperity, however, is that God's blessings must be used to help others. Deuteronomy 15:10–11 says, "Give generously . . . and do so without a grudging heart; then because of this the Lord your God will bless you in all your work and in everything you put your hand to." The book of Proverbs—written during the time of Solomon, one of history's wealthiest rulers—similarly presents wealth as a desirable blessing that can be obtained through hard work, wisdom, and following God's laws. Proverbs 14:31 promises, "The faithless will be fully repaid for their ways, and the good man rewarded for his."

Numerous stories and folktales show the generosity of the patriarchs. According to Jewish legend, Job owned an inn at a crossroads, where he allowed travelers to eat and drink at no cost. When they offered to pay, he instead told them about God, explaining that he was simply a steward of the wealth that God had given to him and urging them to worship God, obey God's commands, and receive their own blessings. A story about Abraham says that when he moved his flocks from one field to another, he would muzzle the animals so that they would not graze on a neighbor's property.

After the death of Solomon, however, the kingdom of Israel

was divided and the people fell away from the commandments God had mandated. The later writings of the prophets, who are attempting to correct misbehavior, specifically address unethical acts committed to gain wealth. "You trample on the poor," complained the prophet Amos. "You oppress the righteous and take bribes and you deprive the poor of justice in the courts" (Amos 5:11, 12). The prophet Isaiah insists, "Learn to do right! Seek justice, encourage the oppressed. . . . If you are willing and obedient, you will eat the best from the land; but if you resist and rebel, you will be devoured by the sword" (Isaiah 1:17, 19–20).

Viewed in this light, the teachings of Jesus take on new meaning. Jesus does not condemn wealth; he condemns those who would allow the pursuit of wealth to come ahead of the proper relationship with God: "No one can serve two masters. . . . You cannot serve both God and money" (Matthew 6:24).

Today, nearly everyone living in the Western world could be considered materially wealthier than the people of the Bible, who had no running water or electricity, lived in tents, walked when traveling long distances, and wore clothing handmade from animal skins. But we also live in an age when tabloid newspapers and trashy television programs avidly follow the misadventures of spoiled and selfish millionaire athletes and entertainers. In the mainstream news outlets, it is common to read or hear reports of corporate greed and malfeasance, or of corrupt politicians enriching themselves at the expense of their constituents. Often, the responsibility of the wealthy to those members of the community who are not as successful seems to have been forgotten.

The purpose of the series MONEY AT ITS BEST: MILLIONAIRES OF THE BIBLE is to examine the lives of key figures from biblical history, showing how these people used their wealth or their powerful and privileged positions in order to make a difference in the lives of others.

The Spanish master Bartolome Esteban Murillo created this 17th-century painting of Job in despair. The lesson of the story of Job is to maintain faith in God even when God seems to deliver unjustified suffering.

OVERVIEW

Job is possibly the most misunderstood person in biblical history, and his story has enraged, mystified, and comforted readers for centuries. The tale of a man who suffers great tragedy for no apparent reason, and yet continue to praise God—even in the midst of his suffering—demonstrates a faith that few people can testify to achieving.

Scholars and critics continue to make attempts to understand the reasoning for Job's suffering and God's purpose for traumatizing his faithful servant. According to Susan E. Schreiner, "Job belongs to the West; his story has captivated the human imagination and has forced its readers to wrestle with the most painful realities of human existence." But Job does not simply belong to the Western world; his plight is a universal one. His story is accessible to whoever reads it.

The chronicle of Job is explored in literature, art, and various religious texts in order to gain insight into the heavily enigmatic tale of a just man who is treated unfairly by the God he worships. Its puzzling nature crosses boundaries of genre, culture, and religion. A great deal of drama and controversy, history and myth, trauma and testimony are packed into the 42 biblical chapters that make up the book of Job.

Much of what is known about Job is found in spiritual texts such as the Hebrew and Christian Bible, the Qur'an, and the Talmud. Many details of Job's life remain ambiguous within those texts. What readers are given in the story is a snapshot into his life, a glimpse into his prosperity and an account of his suffering. As Steven J. Lawson asserts:

> Here is the inspired record of a man who [is] taken to the depths of despair and, by the grace of God, [comes] forth as gold. Here is encouragement for all saints who are facing extreme difficulty and despair. Contained in the account of Job is hope for all who trust God to patiently endure the storm-tossed trials of the soul.

AUTHORSHIP OF THE BOOK OF JOB

One issue concerning the story of Job is establishing the time period in which it was written. Definitive dating of the story depends on who wrote it; however, scholars have yet to authenticate the person behind the text.

It is possible that Job writes the tale himself. He lives well over 100 years after his trial and therefore has plenty of time to pen the narrative. We can assume he tells the story often to those in the community who were witness to his seeming fall from grace—not as a cautionary tale, but as a story of God's divine goodness. If Job was not the

Illustration of Moses, depicted here as the author of the first five books of the Bible: Genesis, Exodus, Leviticus, Numbers, and Deuteronomy. Some scholars believe that Moses may have written the Book of Job as well, because it depicts events that occurred during the Patriarchal period. Job may have been a contemporary of Abraham or his children, which would place his lifetime around 2100 B.C.E. The date of Moses' life is uncertain, but many scholars believe he lived around 1500 B.C.E.

author, then anyone present at the scene of the drama may be dubbed the author. Due to the detailed retelling, it is also possible that one of Job's friends wrote the narrative after Job was healed. "If so this would make Job the most ancient book in the Bible, predating the writing of the Pentateuch," says Lawson.

Jewish tradition attributes authorship of the book of Job to Moses. If this is the case, the book of Job may have been written before the events of the Exodus occurred, possibly during the years Moses wandered in the desert as a shepherd.

The book of Job may also have been written after the establishment of the Kingdom of Israel. Some traditions attribute Job to King Solomon, or a member of his royal court. "[Some scholars advance] Solomon as the writer of this inspired book, mainly because of the similarities among Job and Proverbs, Ecclesiastes, and the Song of Solomon about the poetic literature, Hebrew parallelism, and wisdom literature," notes Lawson. If Solomon is determined to be the book's author, then the dating would likely be during "the day of kings, around 950 B.C.," according to Lawson. However, while the text certainly follows a poetic arrangement, that is not necessarily enough evidence to definitively attribute authorship to Solomon.

DID JOB EXIST?

To add further scrutiny to the debate, some scholars believe that Job never existed; accordingly his story is a fable serving only as a means to teach its readers about the glory of God. According to Thomas Long of Princeton Theological Seminary, "Part folk tale, part epic poem, part Platonic-style dialogue, Job is a jumble of genres, and historical critics are quick to point out that the present form seems to have resulted from the work of a rather heavy set of editorial hands."

Critical studies by Marvin Pope and Georg Fohrer date the book of Job from the fifth to the third centuries b.c.e., alleging "the Joban legend passed through perhaps four stages, evolving from 1.) a pre-Israelite tale; 2.) a pre-exilic version dating from the ninth-eighth centuries B.C.E.; 3.) an exilic version in which the Deuteronomic phraseology was added; and 4.) the postexilic version in which the figure of Satan and elements of Wisdom teaching were incorporated."

The Documentary Hypothesis

According to a longstanding tradition among Christians and Jews, Moses is the author of at least five books in the Bible. However, contemporary scholars generally agree that the Bible is the work of four distinct authors or groups of authors who compiled and edited material from different locations and sources over a period of centuries.

During the late 19th century, a theory of biblical authorship called the Documentary Hypothesis was formulated. Over the years there have been numerous variations on this theory. In its simplest form, the Documentary Hypothesis says that the main blocks of stories in the books of Genesis and Exodus—including the story of Noah—are the oldest material. They are attributed to two anonymous authors, known as J and E. The initials come from the names for God that each author uses in the narrative —J for "Yahweh" (in German, "Jahweh") and E for "Elohim." Scholars believe these two sets of stories were written down between 950 and 800 B.C.E., although they probably existed in oral form much earlier than that.

Around 600 B.C.E., new material concerned with religious or legal matters—such as the covenant between God and Abraham in Genesis 17, along with genealogical information—was added. This material is believed to have been the work of a priest or group of priests, and is labeled P.

The first five books of the Bible (referred to by Jews as the Torah) were placed in their final form around 400 B.C.E. by a group of editors, who blended the J, E, and P strands together and added new material. The addition is labeled R, after the group of redactors who concentrated on reworking and polishing the text.

Over the past two centuries the Biblical text has been the subject of intense scholarly scrutiny. This theory offers an understanding of how the book of Genesis might have been composed. However, there are still numerous points of disagreement among scholars, and many of them may be impossible to ever resolve.

Whether crafted by a skilled individual or based on the life of an actual person, the narrative is undoubtedly compelling and thought provoking, taking its readers along a journey of pain and eventual triumph. What lies between the prologue and epilogue are chapters that resemble the likes of a Shakespearean stage drama interspersed with lines of unyielding poetic intrigue. The writer weaves a tale that allows readers to take on Job's concerns, arousing pity for his plight and apprehension about the possibility of them being unduly punished as well.

JOB IN OTHER SOURCES

Another fascinating tale of the Job story is found within the Apocrypha, a group of texts considered to be unfounded in terms of accuracy and authorship (also known as the pseudepigrapha). The Testament of Job tells a story that is significantly different from the biblical narrative. In the Testament, Job is a king in Egypt. This rendition establishes Job as more than a wealthy landowner; he is a powerful man in charge of ruling a land. It is not clear whether Job is a king by birth or if God blesses him with a kingdom after his trial. The narrative commences with Job chronicling his riches to rags story to his "new" sons and daughters. The story he tells begins much like a folktale as he instructs them to gather close so they may hear his tale.

> The Greek word *apocrypha* means "hidden," and is used to refer to ancient texts that contain religious stories or themes but are not generally considered a part of the Bible. While some apocryphal books have been included in the Roman Catholic Bible since the 16th century, Jews and Protestants do not accept them as divinely inspired scripture.

Indeed, he has quite a story to tell, which may spare his children the same sorrow he endures for a time. It is in the Testament that Job clearly identifies his lineage in the fifth verse, saying:

> For I am of the sons of Esau. My brother is Nahor, and your mother is Dinah. By her have I become your father (Testament of Job 1:5).

While the validity of this text is unsubstantiated by some biblical scholars, this version makes a clear assertion about who Job really is by affirming his ancestry.

The fabled nature of the story is marked in the Jewish faith as well. In the Hebrew Bible (Tanakh) the book of Job (Sefer Iyov) is found in its third book, the Ketuvim, which means "the writing" or "hagiographa." It is considered one of three books of poetry (Sifrei Emet), along with Psalms and Proverbs. According to the Jewish faith, the Sefer Iyov is allegorical in nature.

In the Chumash, a collection of the five books written by Moses, also known as the Pentateuch or Torah, the Sefer Iyov outlines the depths of human suffering and the struggle for faith in Hashem (God). While speculation still surrounds the authorship of the work, it is most commonly believed by many Hebrew scholars to have been written by Moses in the desire to understand the meaning of suffering.

Identifying Moses as the author of the book in many ways authenticates the parallels that can be drawn between him and Job. Much like Job, Moses is also chosen by God to suffer. As Jonathan Kirsch points out, "Moses may have been God's chosen one, the man whom God revealed his secret name and the physical manifestation of his 'glory,' the man whom God knew 'face to face,' the man with whom he would speak 'mouth to mouth, as a friend speaketh to a friend"—and yet Moses was also the man whom God stalked and sought to kill."

The Islamic holy book, the Qur'an, also recounts the story of Job, or Ayyub. In this version, Job is a descendent of Isaac, who is the son of Abraham. The suffering Job endures in the Qur'an is similar to biblical accounts. In times of hardship the Qur'an instructs its followers to remember Job and his patience during moments of trials. Job teaches that patience and piety receive reward in the end. Job is considered one of Islam's great prophets.

Still another analysis of Job's fall is that it vindicates God's goodness and justice in the face of the existence of evil. Satan's purpose is simply to cause strife and bring pain into the world. But even though Satan runs rampant, Job's story allows the reader to witness God in control. Lawson points out,

> God is seen reigning sovereignly over man's suffering as he appoints it for his own glory. Further, God is seen using Satan in inflicting the pain of the righteous. In all this, the Book of Job upholds the blameless character of God, affirming his sovereign right to do whatever he pleases.

The book of Job is more than just a story addressing the theological question surrounding the suffering of the righteous and the prosperity of the wicked, but also, if not most importantly, the sovereign power of God. How God chooses to wield that power plays out to the limit in Job's story. At times, God's methods of exercising this power may appear extreme. However, they serve a holy purpose that is beyond comprehension. In the conclusion we get a glimpse of God's dominance, which is undeniable. And whether considered parable or history, scholars continue

Qur'an 21:83 reads, "And Job, when he cried out to his Lord: 'Adversity has afflicted me while You are the most Merciful of the Mercy-granting!' We responded to him and removed any adversity he was facing, and we gave him his household and the same as them besides, as a Mercy from Our presence and a Reminder for worshipers." The passage clearly addresses concerns about enduring suffering. As long as an afflicted individual follows Ayyub's (Job's) example and continues to praise Allah, says the Islamic scripture, he or she will inevitably receive compensation.

to struggle to comprehend the fairness of his rule in the case of Job.

Moshe ben Maimon (or Maimonides), the medieval Jewish philosopher and rabbi, writes in the *Guide of the Perplexed* his view of the story of Job as "'a parable intended to set forth the opinions of people concerning providence' in response to the apparent affliction of a 'righteous and perfect man' with grievous misfortune." Because of a general belief in God's divine providence, Job not only loves God, but is fearful of him as well. Job's suffering is justified because he is brought closer to God and comes to an understanding of God's divinity by the end of his trial. It is the belief of Maimonides that as a parable, the story of Job is therefore "intended to set forth the opinions of people concerning providence. . . . The suffering of people like Job, Maimonides says, raises the issue of 'God's knowledge and His providence' and throws people into doubt about whether there is any order in human affairs." Maimonides' analysis allows for the philosophical question concerning whether Job's knowledge of God validates his suffering great losses, including the death of his children. And for some readers the suffering that Job endures is too great to be explained away in these terms. It may appear that understanding God's providence lacks substance in the face of undue affliction.

Moshe ben Nahman Gerondi, more commonly known as Nahmanides, also offers commentary on the tale, but approaches Job from a mystical standpoint. As a Catalan rabbi, Nahmanides believes Job is punished by God because of heresy. Job's long-endured suffering continues and escalates in severity simply because he believes God is wrong in his initial punishment of him. Job knows he has done nothing wrong; he is outraged because he does everything right. While Nahmanides respects Maimonides, he does not agree with his views on the condition of Job. In his commentary he writes:

> Wisdom is hidden from humans. All that God [reveals] to them is that they ought to fear Him and shun evil. But their reward and punishment, the security of the wicked and the torments of the righteous—these are not matters that are revealed to humans. Job cannot discern any justice in them, nor does he attain any wisdom on the topic from his friends.

For Nahmanides, Job is seemingly at the pinnacle of power when he is visited by a misfortune that cannot be understood and will not be explained.

In discussing Job's tribulation, J. H. Eaton describes his story as "a world ruled by a God intent on justice, the most just of men has been placed, at God's decision, in an abyss of protracted suffering, his happiness shattered by bereavement, disease and degradation." Job is instantly thrust into a God-approved lifestyle that is foreign to him. Nothing of the narrative claims that Job has undergone any form of suffering before this moment. Job has been, it seems, under a protective cloak of blessings for the majority of his life. Nothing has prepared him for the torment he is to experience at Satan's hands and with God's approval.

APPEAL OF THE JOB STORY TODAY

Whether Job's world is a creation of an unnamed writer or a retelling of actual events, the story continues to elicit dialogue. Those who believe the narrative to be a fabrication point to the structure of the book of Job as a way to prove that it is fiction. As J. H. Eaton claims, "The Prologue and Epilogue remind us of folk-stories, with repetition of wording, symmetry of event, the uncomplicated perfection of Job, and attention to details such as the numbers of the herds and the children." This style is reminiscent of many modern fables, with a tidy exposition and a conclusion in which the main characters are rewarded for their time of peril. The story commences neatly; everything is resolved. Job's story shares many of the traditional characteristics of the genre: the clear difference between good and evil or what is right and wrong, the generic location of "the land," the tests the protagonist must undergo, and finally, the happy ending. Because the story is structured to resemble a folktale, readers expect to encounter a moral or message behind its telling. Whether meant to be a story of instructions on how to endure all things or a cautionary tale describing what could befall the sinfully wicked, the biblical book of Job chronicles one man's enduring struggle of reason versus faith.

Undoubtedly, the overwhelming issue that continues to plague readers is the timeless question, Why do good people suffer? The question cannot be posited as a blanket fact asserting all innocent men suffer, but rather must be considered in the context of the story. The theme of Job's story, as author William Henry Green asserts, is "the case of piety without prosperity, or the righteousness of God exercised toward faithful sufferers." Can faithfulness be proved if one has none of the accouterments of wealth and the protection of health? Another question that arises in Job's story is whether humans have the right or authority to question God's actions. In the midst of his suffering Job cries out, inquiring as to why God has set his eye on him. In essence Job believes God singles him out for some unknown reason and wonders why God is picking on him. In the Bava Batra, the third of the three tractates in the Talmud, this line of questioning is seen as blasphemous behavior.

But Job's life is not all tragedy. Within this text we will discuss his life in three major periods: the suffering of an innocent man, his response to his suffering, and the lessons he learns from his suffering. His story is compact. Little is written about the man before or after he becomes a pawn in a wager between God and Satan. But he obviously lives a prosperous and meaningful life before and after the events that befall him in a land called Uz.

Job's Life and Status

The biblical account of Job's life begins like a traditional folktale: "There was a man in the land of Uz, whose name was Job; and that man was perfect and upright, and one that feared God and eschewed evil" (Job 1:1). In this opening sentence the reader is thrust into the life of Job. No information is given regarding his lineage at this point. Some scholars have hypothesized that Job is the same person as Jobab, a man named earlier in the book of Genesis who is the son of Zerah from Bozrah and the king of Edom. What we do know about Job from these lines is that he is a wholly pious individual and a man of great riches.

The text goes on to say: "He had seven sons and three daughters, and he owned seven thousand sheep, three thousand camels, five hundred yoke of oxen and five hundred donkeys, and had a large number of servants. He was the greatest man among all the people of the East" (Job

1:2–3). From the start Job is set apart from others in his area, and his presence obviously looms large in this area. It is important to ascertain the location of Job's homeland in order to understand the role he plays within the community.

Determining the exact location of the land of Uz is as challenging as determining the existence of Job himself. Since the book of Job does not give factual evidence as to the exact locale where he lives, one must deduce the location from the hints given throughout the book as well as other places within the Bible. This location is mentioned in only two other places in the Bible. Jeremiah 25:20 states, "and all the foreign people there; all the kings of Uz," and Lamentations 4:21 says, "Rejoice and be glad, O Daughter of Edom, you who lived in the land of Uz." It is

Job's Life and Status 25

speculated that the land may have been named after Uz, the son of Aram, in chapter 10 of Genesis:

> Unto Shem also, the father of all the children of Eber, the brother of Japheth the elder, even to him were children born. The children of Shem; Elam, and Asshur, and Arphaxad, and Lud, and Aram. And the children of Aram; Uz, and Hul, and Gether, and Mash. (Genesis 10:21–23)

Later, 1 Chronicles states, "The sons of Shem; Elam, and Asshur, and Arphaxad, and Lud, and Aram, and Uz, and Hul, and Gether, and Meshech" (1 Chronicles 1:17). From the opening lines in the book of Job, it can only be said that he lives in the eastern region of the world.

The land of Uz may have been located east of the Sea of Galilee, pictured here.

John Gill, an English Baptist theologian and Calvinist, provides information on Job's place of origin, saying, "We read of the land of Uz along with Edom, or rather of Edom as in the land of Uz, or on the borders of it, the *Targum* calls it the land of Armenia, but rather it is Arabia; and very probably it was one of the Arabias Job lived in, either Petraea or Deserta, probably the latter." The Arabian location is considered the present-day northwestern Saudi Arabia. The more likely location of Uz is east of the Sea of Galilee and south of Damascus, which today is western Jordan or southern Syria. Positioned within this land, the history of Edom provides the reader with additional information into the distinctive character of Job. As if taking on the temperament of its founder, Esau, some biblical histories allege that the Edomites are known to be an untamed, godless race of people. If this is an accurate depiction of his countrymen, then it is a remarkable show of character for Job to live in such an environment and yet retain his faithfulness.

Job's story takes place during the middle Bronze Age, otherwise known as the patriarchal period, which spans the years 2000 B.C.E. to 1500 B.C.E. In this time period, Job is perhaps one of the wealthiest landowners in his area. In terms of economics, "wealth was measured primarily in terms of land, animals, and servants; and Job had all three in abundance." God has blessed him with animals numbering in the thousands, and the necessary lands to lodge and feed them stretches out for miles. He is not only blessed economically, but also with a large family that includes 10 children. Job sets an example of how wealth and social approval are symbols of God's holy blessings being bestowed upon man. According to the dominantly held belief system of the patriarchal period, God rewards those who are good. One only needs to know or come into

A shepherd walks with his herd in modern-day Israel. In the ancient world of the Bible, ownership of livestock represented great wealth.

contact with Job to realize that God has most certainly found favor in him. Job's story provides an understanding of how lucratively God blesses him for his faithfulness.

In terms of wealth, Job easily stands out among other landowners. His sheep provide a large amount of wool for clothing for the family and to be sold for profit. The camels are not only beneficial for carrying items and travel, but they also produce a large quantity of milk. We can assume that Job uses the camels for transporting trade goods to increase his wealth. Oxen and donkeys are used as work animals to plough and maintain his considerable acreage. The total amount of his landholdings, animals, and slaves is characteristic of the wealth exhibited of kings and princes in the eastern regions.

Gold bracelets, a flower-headed pin, and an onyx vase from the tomb of a Syrian princess, circa 1700 B.C.E.

Scripture also indicates that Job's children live a rather lavish lifestyle. Job's sons throw large feasts at their individual homes and invite their sisters along. After a feast, Job rises early in the morning to ritually purify his children. He burns an offering in their names with the belief that during the celebration they may have "sinned and cursed God in their hearts" (Job 1:5). The narrative states that Job does this on a regular basis. From this deed we can assume that his children did little with their inherited riches other than enjoy them. There are no other reports of their actions throughout the narrative other than taking pleasure in food and drink. Because they exhibit this spoiled, rich-kid mentality, the responsibility for their salvation falls on the shoulders of their father. It is not apparent whether Job attends any of the lavish affairs, but what is known, or assumed, is that perhaps there is errant behavior occurring during the evening. Job is diligent and devoted to his children's well-being, and so he takes up their cause daily, possibly fearing God's punishment.

The Testament of Job does speak at length about not only Job's riches, but what he does with them. He uses his wealth to aid those less fortunate than himself. The Testament states:

> For I had one hundred and thirty thousand sheep, and of these I separated seven thousand for the clothing of orphans and widows and of needy and sick ones. I had a herd of eight hundred dogs who watched my sheep and besides these two hundred to watch my house. And I had nine mills working for the whole city and ships to carry goods, and I sent them into every city and into the villages to the feeble and sick and to those that were unfortunate. And I had three hundred and forty thousand nomadic asses, and of these I set aside five hundred, and the offspring of these I order to be sold and the proceeds to be given to the poor and the needy. For from all the lands the poor came to meet me. For the four doors of my house were opened, each, being in charge of a watchman who had to see whether there were any people coming asking alms, and whether they would see me sitting at one of the doors so that they could leave through the other and take whatever they needed. I also had thirty immovable tables set at all hours for the strangers alone, and I also had twelve tables spread for the widows. And if any one came asking for alms, he found food on my table to take all he needed, and I turned nobody away to leave my door with an empty stomach. I also had three thousand five hundred yokes of oxen, and I selected of these five hundred and had them tend to the plowing. And with these I had done all the work in

each field by those who would, take it in charge and the income of their crops I laid aside for the poor on their table. I also had fifty bakeries from which I sent [the bread] to the table for the poor. (Testament of Job 3:1–11)

Job's willingness to give whatever he has to whoever is in need characterizes him as a man who is devoutly concerned with his fellow citizens. His concern is the well-being of those living in or visiting the city. He also describes how he releases many men from the debt they owe him. Job lays these facts out in an attempt to call attention to his goodness. He has done right by God in terms of his blessings; it is important for people to know this fact.

According to Jewish rabbinical literature, Job's great wealth is not only economic, but also in great wisdom. In this literature, Job is one of Pharaoh's three advisors. One night Pharaoh has a nightmare regarding Egyptian elders being "weighed against a 'sucking lamb' on the scales of justice, and the frail suckling outweighed them." Pharaoh is confused by the dream and calls his advisors to his side to decipher the hidden meaning. Job is called upon to assist Pharaoh during trying times. In his article "And Iyov Was Silent," Rabbi Eli Teitelbaum writes about Job:

> He helped support every good and worthy cause. He gave charity to all that needed his help. He was a wise and clever man who was always ready to help those in need. He was a man of great moral character who always distanced himself from anything that might lead to sin. He was a multimillionaire who owned much real estate all over the world and was blessed with a large family and everything that one's heart desired. He was what we'd call 'healthy wealthy and wise."

Job uses his wisdom to consult Pharaoh concerning what should be done about the increasing population of Israelites in Egypt. One of the advisors instructs Pharaoh to kill them; another argues in their defense. But Job decides to say nothing. Whether Job makes a wise decision in this case is unclear. What is certain is that his wisdom is such that he is elevated to advisor, which sets him apart from other men in the region.

These renderings offer a glimpse of an extraordinary man by all accounts. Job is not characterized as an average man by any means. He is almost larger than life in terms of his wealth, wisdom, and piety. As Thomas G. Long states:

> Like Paul Bunyan, Job is the tallest and the strongest and the best, and thus does not evoke an existential connection with the plight of the human beings in the audience. He stands at some distance from the ordinary round of human life. At this point, Job is not "everyman," he is "superman."

And as author Alan Cooper maintains:

> The transformation of Job into an Everyman, the prototype for all innocent sufferers, is one of the great feats in the history of biblical interpretation. The reason is not far to seek: most people presumably consider their suffering to be undeserved. Like Job, they seek an explanation that gives meaning to their lives while simultaneously absolving them of blame. And all people hope that their suffering will reach the same happy conclusion as Job's—health, family, and fortune restored, evidently none the worse for wear.

Even though he is portrayed in this common-man way, Job's unyielding piety and his overwhelming wealth posi-

An Advisor to Pharaoh

A Jewish tradition holds that Job was an advisor to the Pharaoh during the time that the Israelites were enslaved in Egypt. The Israelites had been invited to settle in Egypt by an earlier ruler, but his successor feared their growing numbers. This Pharaoh orders the Israelites to be enslaved, and they endure great losses due to their forced enslavement. But the Biblical narrative states that the more the Israelites were oppressed, the more their population grew.

"To punish Pharaoh for his cruelty toward the children of Israel, God afflicted him with a plague of leprosy, which covered his whole body," writes the Jewish scholar Louis Ginzberg in his collection of folklore *Legends of the Jews*. "[Pharaoh] took counsel with his three advisors, Balaam, Jethro, and Job, how he might be healed of the awful malady that had seized upon him. Balaam spoke, saying, 'Thou canst regain thy health only if thou wilt slaughter Israelitish children and bathe in their blood.' Jethro, averse from having a share in such an atrocity, left the king and fled to Midian. Job, on the other hand, though he also disapproved of Balaam's counsel, kept silence, and in no wise protested against it, wherefore God punished him with a year's suffering. But afterward He loaded [Job] down with all the felicities of this life, and granted him many years, so that this pious Gentile might be rewarded in this world for his good deeds."

The Israelites continue working in slavery until Moses leads them out of Egypt.

tion him apart from the other members of society. Job stands as a model of how the people of his community should live. And while he is in many ways admired for these qualities, he also resides in a position that detaches him from the community and will, therefore, garner him little sympathy from his peers once he is afflicted.

The book of Job stands as a timeless tale of human suffering and redemption. People can interpret the story with a critical eye or put themselves into the story. As Cynthia Ozick confirms, "Because [Job] is unidentified by period or place, nothing in his situation is foreign or obsolete; his story cannot blunder into anachronism or archaism."

Later Job details his status in society by reflecting on how good his life had been before his suffering. "How I long for the months gone by, for the days when God watched over me, when his lamp shone upon my head and by his light I walked through darkness! Oh, for the days when I was in my prime, when God's intimate friendship blessed my house, when the Almighty was still with me, when my path was drenched with cream and the rock poured out for me streams of olive oil" (Job 29:2–6). Job's longing for the "good old days" also gives the reader a glimpse further into his personality. He delights in his fortune, almost revels in the blessing bestowed upon him, deriving pleasure from his wealth and what he is able to accomplish with it. The reference of the rock pouring forth olive oil is reminiscent of a passage in Psalms 81:16 regarding those who trust in the Lord: "But you would be fed with the finest of wheat; with honey from the rock I would satisfy you." According to this passage it is clear that God has the ability to sustain those who follow his will, and they should never want, for God can bestow blessings from even the most lifeless of things. Job remembers and mourns for a time when he was in God's favor and was protected by him. Knowledge of that protection allows him to walk the streets of the town and feel as if he is a powerful man.

The general public respects Job, as can be seen in this passage: "When I went to the gate of the city and took my seat in the public square, the young men saw me and stepped aside and the old men rose to their feet; the chief men refrained from speaking and covered their mouths with their hands; the voices of the nobles were hushed, and their tongues stuck to the roof of their mouths" (Job 29:7–10). Job's wealth affords him a revered station in society. In this depiction we see a very different Job. This does not seem to be the same pious man who shuns evil. This individual is one who welcomes attention and outwardly flaunts his wealth and status the wealth affords. But Job quickly restricts this view by relating the facts of the good that he did with his wealth. Before his wealth is stripped away, Job asserts that he used his fortune for good and not evil. Job attests, "Whoever heard of me spoke well of me, and those who saw me commended me, because I rescued the poor who cried out for help, and the fatherless who had none to assist him" (Job 29:11). He goes on to say, "I was a father to the needy" (Job 29:16). Job has a rather high opinion of himself. He seems to view himself on the same plane as God. Much like God bringing forth nourishment from the rock for those in need, Job produces sustenance for the disadvantaged people of his town.

MUCH IS TESTED

In the narrative Job is going about his daily life, praising God and doing no wrong. As a result, he avoids the "evil eye" of Satan, the fallen angel who wages war with God for the souls of humankind.

In the Hebrew Bible the word *ha-Satan* is used as the title of the fallen angel, meaning "the adversary" or "obstacle." Ha-Satan is powerless on earth unless humans commit wicked deeds; when they do, he is quick to point out mankind's evil deeds to God. He is seemingly free to wander the world in search of individuals to slander and ridicule in the face of God. However, despite the apparent "freedom" that Satan has to roam and stalk his prey, he must still report to God along with the other angels, giving accounts of his journeys. William Henry Green points out, "There is a superior restraint to which he is obliged to bow, a superior will that sets limits to his rage, and allows him even within these limits to

The Adversary

Satan's biblical role is to tempt and to sway people from the right path. The Bible opens with the story of Adam and Eve as an account of humans' fall from grace. Satan takes the form of a serpent and is called "more crafty than any of the wild animals" (Genesis 3:1). In this guise he is able to lead Eve astray. In another instance, at the Last Supper Jesus mentions that Satan is still on the prowl for people to destroy and notifies his disciple, "Simon, Simon, Satan has asked to sift you as wheat. But I have prayed for you, Simon, that your faith may not fail" (Luke 22:31).

This Swiss fresco depicts the serpent (Satan) tempting Adam and Eve.

Satan is known by many names throughout biblical history. In the book of Job, when he is not speaking to God, Job makes reference to the devil while cursing the day he was born, saying, "May those who curse days curse that day, those who are ready to rouse Leviathan" (Job 3:8). We also read of Satan being referred to as a leviathan in Isaiah: "In that day, the Lord will punish with his sword, his fierce, great and powerful sword, Leviathan the gliding serpent, Leviathan the coiling serpent; he will slay the monster of the sea" (Isaiah 27:1). And while it seems that man has no chance against the wiles of the Adversary, the Bible clearly states that faith in the divine can triumph over evil. Ephesians reads: "Finally, be strong in the Lord and in his mighty power. Put on the full armor of God so that you can take your stand against the devil's schemes" (Ephesians 6:10).

act on his evil nature only for the sake of some divine end, which he is made to be instrumental in achieving."

What is surprisingly made clear is that God offers up Job for Satan's consideration. In this regard an unnerving question arises: Why did God bring attention to Job? According to Lawson:

> Job was deeply rooted in his faith in God; and when the highly charged storm of adversity hit, Job was a lightning rod who drew the fire. Tragedy came not because there was anything wrong in his life but, to the contrary, because everything was right. He was the most righteous man on the earth, and thus he was marked to suffer.

Job is the perfect candidate for God to allow Satan to test. Because if someone who is without blame is taken down to the lowest position and still continues to praise God in the midst of his suffering, then one can assume others will be able to do the same. According to the Testament of Job, Satan is so incensed by Job's benevolence that he "demand[s] the warfare of God against [him]" (Testament of Job 4:7). The purpose behind Job's trial, in the mind of Satan, is to pull his eyes and heart away from the worship of God.

Understanding why God offers up his man, Job, is not easy. Those who believe in God's omnipotence would certainly question the idea that God was unaware of the result. God accepts the challenge not because he does not know how it will turn out, but because he does know the outcome and wants to prove what he already knows to Satan. The test that Job undergoes then is not pointless; to the contrary, it serves a divine purpose. According to John Calvin, the very essence of Christian life is one of suffering; Calvin compares the trials that Job experiences to

In his theological writings, John Calvin (1509–1564) emphasized God's rule over all things. "For whomever the Lord has adopted and deemed worthy of his fellowship ought to prepare themselves for a hard, toilsome, and unquiet life, crammed with very many and various kinds of evil," Calvin wrote. "Why should we exempt ourselves, therefore, from the condition to which Christ our Head had to submit, especially since he submitted to it for our sake to show us an example of patience in himself?"

other biblical figures, David and Jesus, and says that the suffering of these righteous men is "preeminent proof that God afflicts those whom he loves." By reading the story of Job, therefore, people can get an understanding of the proper way to endure trials and how to remain faithful during times of great distress.

When God asks Satan, "Have you considered my servant Job? There is no one on earth like him; he is blameless and upright, a man who fears God and shuns evil" (Job 1:8), he issues Satan the perfect person to investigate. God believes Job is a perfect example, but Satan does not. By setting Job up as a model individual, it is as if Satan cannot help but test his righteousness. Satan believes Job to be guilty of false piety. Satan's query lies not in Job's actions, for it is clear that Job is devoted to God, but rather in his motivations. Why is Job so committed to God? Satan claims that God has blessed Job so much so that he has no reason to turn against him. Remaining safe under God's care, Job is reasonably pious. According to Green, Satan sees Job's dedication to God as "a refined form of selfishness." Satan believes that Job is not good for the sake of being good, but that it serves his purposes to remain faithful. According to Satan, God merely has to "stretch out [his] hand and strike everything that [Job] has, and he will surely curse [God] to [his] face" (Job 1:11).

Beyond the obvious indictment of Job, Satan is also pointing the finger at God. He charges God to be a manipulator who is not worthy of Job's, or anyone else's, praise; therefore, God must pay for it. As Warren W. Wiersbe lays out, it is as if Satan says:

> The only reason Job fears You is because You pay him to do it. You two have made a contract: You protect him and prosper him as long as he obeys and worships You. You are not a God worthy of worship! You have to pay people to honor You.

Satan sets a challenge before God; who better to take up this charge than his faithful servant, Job. God knows that he is not likely to disappoint.

The questions arise: Would man continue to serve God if he had nothing? Is faithfulness dependent on reward? God does not believe this to be true. God believes people are truly devoted because he is the Almighty, not for what they may receive. According to Green, Satan's issue concerns "whether there is such a thing as real godliness in the earth, a godliness that is not merely self-seeking, but which heartily loves the right and cleaves to it, and chooses the service of God though no hope of profit may be forthcoming." And while God may believe there are people who live by this conduct, especially in the case of Job, it can only be proved with a test. How else can God prove that he will still be worshiped and followed without a trial? He allows Satan to take away Job's riches, even his family, saying, "Very well, then, everything he has is in your hands, but on the man himself do not lay a finger" (Job 1:12). The events that transpire after this bet is made and accepted is, as Long describes, "a scene of high tragicomedy."

Contrary to the widely held view that God grants his permission to strike at Job after Satan has his plan in mind, John Calvin, the Protestant theologian, sees it very differently. Calvin states, "From the first chapter of Job we know that Satan, no less than the angels, who willingly obey, presents himself before God to receive his commands. . . . However, even though a bare permission to afflict the holy man then seems to be added, yet we gather that God is the author of that trial of which Satan and his wicked thieves were the ministers." In this explanation one understands the divine message that God is sending not only to Satan, but to the world. God cannot be persuaded to allow harm to befall his loyal servant; God conceives the idea himself. This gives reasons for God offering Job up as an example of piousness to Satan. If God is omnipotent then he knows Satan is looking for conflict and desires to create disorder in the world. He knows how the trial will end. He knows Job will not curse him. Susan E. Schreiner further explains Calvin's view by adding, "Therefore, although the biblical portrayal of Job raises the specter of a history abandoned by God or a God who torments human beings, Calvin finds in this story an affirmation that God justly and providentially decrees every event in nature and in history." God's plan serves a greater purpose. He knows the outcome. Satan is just trying to keep up. And after the first round, Satan is drawn back to God, defeated.

Although the readers know of the horrendous situation about to affect him, Job is happily ignorant of the bet that

Much Is Tested 41

This 14th century Italian painting shows the Devil (top left) asking God if he can tempt Job. "Now Satan betook himself to God, and prayed Him to put Job into his power," wrote Louis Ginzberg in Legends of the Jews. According to his tale, Satan says, "'As for Job, it is true, I found none that loveth Thee as he does, but if Thou wilt put him into my hand, I shall succeed in turning his heart away from Thee.' But God spake, 'Satan, Satan, what hast thou a mind to do with my servant Job, like whom there is none in the earth?' Satan persisted in his request touching Job, and God granted it. He gave him full power over Job's possessions."

is waged between God and Satan regarding his faithfulness. While the bet is between the two, Alan Cooper claims, "So callous does God appear to be in the prologue that some commentators (notably Martin Buber) have been inclined to argue that the portrayal of the deity there is incongruous and unreal, manifesting an erroneous theology that will be corrected later on." Readers must understand that this is not the scene of an angry God. The significant detail is not that God is allowing Job to be senselessly punished; rather it is the reason why God takes part in the bet and consents to the occurrence of this treatment, a reason that is unveiled as the story progresses.

MOURNING SONG

Readers of the book of Job have the privilege of knowing what tragedy is about to befall Job. We have been privy to the terms of the bet between God and Satan and know that while much will be taken away from Job, his life will be spared. Job suffers great losses at the hand of Satan and with the permission of God. The dark and dangerous hand of Satan has crept into Job's life and makes quick work of his destruction.

Job is going about his daily tasks when one of his servants brings news that his oxen, donkeys, and the servants watching over them have been attacked and taken away by Sabeans. This messenger is the only one left to survive the attack. In the midst of this discussion, another of his servants arrives to tell Job that his sheep and the servants caring for them had been struck down by "the fire of God" (Job 1:16). Another servant enters and explains to Job that his camels were raided by the

Caldeans. The Testament of Job tells that Satan then turns himself into the King of Persia and sets siege upon Uz. Satan declares to the inhabitants of Uz that Job has taken all the resources of their city, leaving them with nothing, and that he has destroyed a temple of God. Finally, another messenger appears and gives Job possibly the toughest news to hear, saying, "Your sons and daughters were feasting and drinking wine at the oldest brother's house, when suddenly a mighty wind swept in from the desert and struck the four corners of the house. It collapsed on them and they are dead" (Job 1:18–19).

As a work of literature, J. H. Eaton notes, "In the account of the messengers we notice the story-teller's skill in combining repetition and climax." With reports on his

Job and his wife tear their clothes after learning about the loss of their fortune and the deaths of their children in this painting from the late 15th century. Keriah, the tearing of a garment, is an expression of grief practiced in the Jewish religion. In the Bible, there are other accounts of people practicing keriah, such as Jacob and David.

lowly domestic animals to the fate of his children, the reader cannot help but be as stunned as Job is upon hearing the tragic information.

Job is instantly thrust into mourning, and he illustrates his sorrow by tearing his robe, shaving his head, falling to the ground, and weeping, "Naked I came from my mother's womb, and naked I will depart" (Job 1:21). This behavior is in keeping with the traditional Jewish custom of keriah. Once a person hears of the passing away of a relative, the mourner is required to rip his clothing or a black ribbon. Explaining the Jewish tradition of mourning, David Abelman asserts,

> The tearing of the garments is not just a symbolic expression of mourning, but a true expression of heartfelt grief. Perhaps this tearing of the garment, more than any other act, expresses the immense feeling of sorrow that the newly bereaved individual has. No words can express this feeling of loss and during the week of "shiva", the mourner continues to wear his torn garment.

Despite these losses, Job still manages to praise the Lord in the same verse, uttering, "The Lord gave and the Lord has taken away; may the name of the Lord be praised" (Job 1:21). He is conscious that the only reason he has received such riches is due to the Lord, and if God has seen fit to take these things from him, than so be it. While in his grief, Job presumably does not understand why all of his blessings have been so cruelly taken away, he does not curse the Lord as Satan has believed.

All the while Job remains faithful in his praise of God. We can assume that Satan is upset by Job's continued piousness. After this initial loss, Satan returns to God and on his second meeting asks God to appraise Job's behavior.

And for the second time, God continues to expound Job's faithfulness by using the same words to describe him as he had earlier in the biblical narrative, calling him "blameless and upright, a man who fears God and shuns evil." God goes on to say, "And he still maintains his integrity, though you incited me against him to ruin him without any reason" (Job 2:3). It is almost as if God is taunting Satan. It is clear that even without his worldly possessions, Job will remain steadfast in his praise.

Realizing that God has allowed him to attack Job previously, Satan knowingly goes after Job once more. Job is strong and fit now; he can recover from these losses, regain wealth, and have other children because he is still able. Surely Job will curse God if his health is taken away from him. "A man will give all he has for his own life. But stretch out your hand and strike his flesh and bones, and he will surely curse you to your face" (Job 2:4–5). Trusting in his loyalty, God again allows the hand of Satan to strike at Job with the understanding that he can do anything but take Job's life. God has set the rules of Job's trial. He can be taken to the brink, his health can be impaired, but his life must be spared. In proving humans' loyalty, God is not ready to lose a faithful follower.

While the narrative does not identify the disease Job is given, his second course of suffering consists of symptoms similar to diseases such as leprosy or a skin cancer, including boils, itching, running sores, fever, and blackened, deadened skin. The primary symptom of those suffering from leprosy is legions to the skin, which can result in further damage to the skin, nerves, extremities, and eyes. Job is covered with painful sores from his head to his feet. He continues to exist in this sickened state for months. In such agonizing pain, Job could do little but sit among the ashes far outside of his community and scrape his sores

Job is depicted with painful skin boils in this 15th century German woodcut. Satan is shown in the background, as are scenes of the destruction of Job's home and family.

with a piece of broken pottery. Leprosy has long had a social stigma surrounding its sufferers. The disease is seen throughout the Bible as the indicator of sin. The book of Leviticus, written by Moses, lays out instructions for a priest on how to examine and determine various skin diseases. Chapter 13 illustrates the plight of the leper:

> The person with such an infectious disease must wear torn clothes, let his hair be unkempt, cover the lower part of his face and cry out, "Unclean! Unclean!" As long as he has the infection he remains unclean. He must live alone; he must live outside the camp. (Leviticus 13:45–46)

While it is not evident that the illness Job suffers from is leprosy, it is doubtless that Job endures ridicule and persecution because he exhibits signs of such a disease. The story does not say whether Job is cast out or if he flees, but he ends up at the edge of town. Describing Job's wretched location, Wiersbe says:

> There the city garbage was deposited and burned, and there the city's rejects lived, begging alms from whoever passed by. At the ash heap, dogs fought over something to eat, and the city's dung was brought and burned. The city's leading citizen was now living in abject poverty and shame.

And while the reader is aware of the fact that Job shaves his head as a sign of mourning, the outside observer might mistake his baldness as a symptom of the disease. Another symptom, which the biblical narrative does not provide, is that Job's body is covered with worms. In Job's telling of the story found in the Testament of Job, he states: "And I wet the earth with the moistness of my sore body, for matter flowed off my body, and many worms covered it. And when a single worm crept off my body, I put it back saying: 'Remain on the spot where thou hast been placed until He who hath sent thee will order thee elsewhere'" (Testament of Job 5:7–8). Whether covered by worms or not, Job undoubtedly is suffering beyond measure. The disease is wrecking havoc on his body, and he can do nothing to ease his pain. He must sit and endure it, contemplating the reason and method of his current state.

But Job's ordeal is not for the mere amusement of Satan. In many ways, Job is a tool. He is used by both Satan and God, but for very different purposes. For Satan, Job serves as an example of a man whose worship is purely for show, a payment for a service rendered by God. If his service is taken away, if he is broken down and striped bare of everything, he no longer has a reason for payment or a need to praise the Lord. But, for God, Job serves a divine purpose. His function is, as Eaton believes, "to see the world's evil honestly and still believe in God." He is proof that God is the Almighty and is not only deserving of praise, but will absolutely receive it regardless of the circumstances. While Job's outward condition is painfully obvious to anyone who looks upon him, his inner turmoil is not in view, but it causes worse damage. How can God, whom Job has so faithfully served, now turn his back on him and cause him such physical and mental pain? This situation refutes all that Job believes about God, a shared belief common to the time in which he lives, that suffering is predicated on a person's sins.

Job's wife cannot bear to see him in such a condition. The biblical narrative says nothing of his wife's feeling regarding the death of her children or the loss of her riches. She does, however, have strong feeling about the suffering of her husband. She would rather he end his torture

50 Job

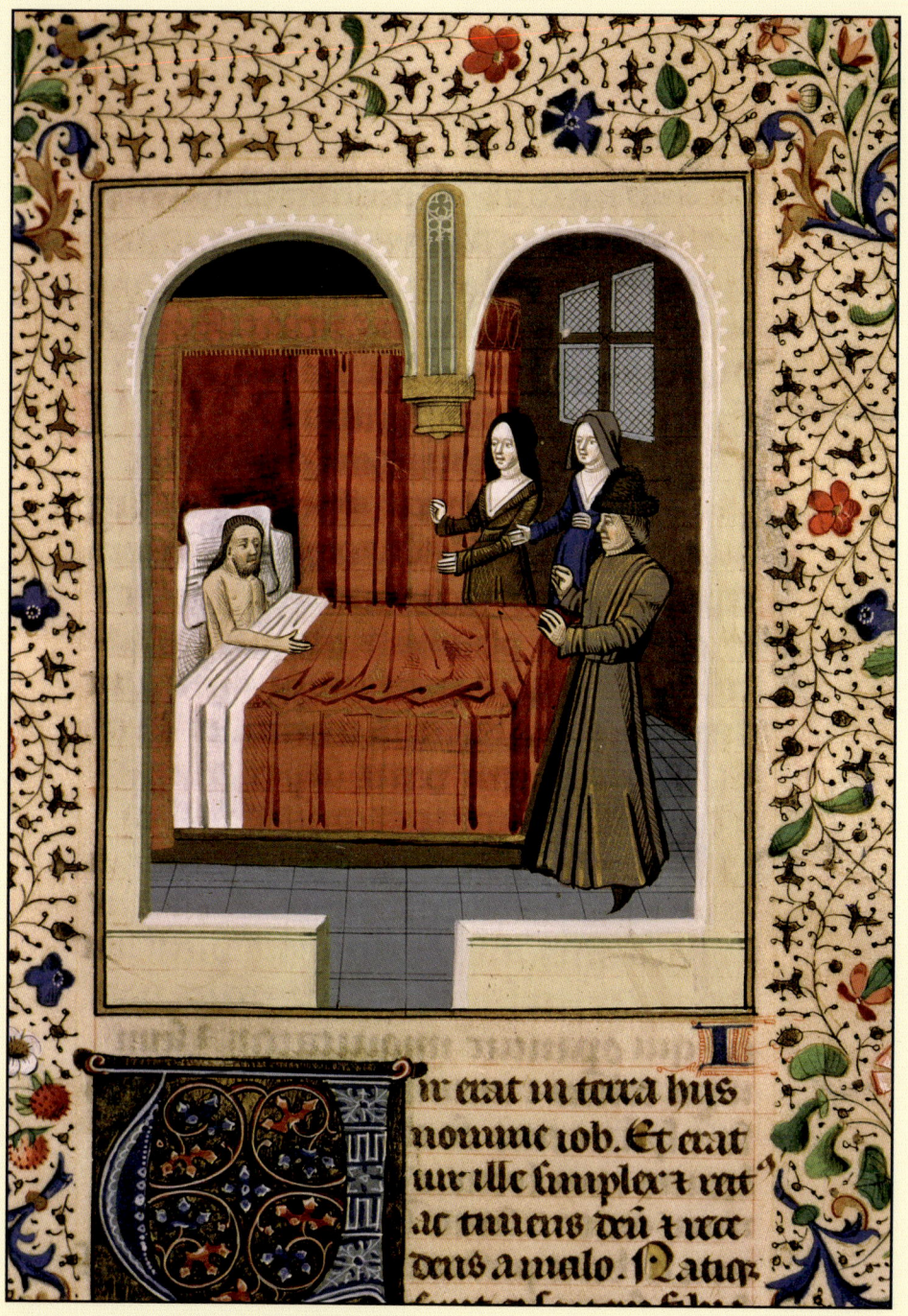

Leprous Job in bed, visited by wife and friends. This illustration is from a 15th century manuscript Bible said to be of Pope John XXII.

in death and urges, "Are you still holding on to your integrity? Curse God and die" (Job 2:9). His wife falls into the trap laid down by Satan. By instructing Job to commit blasphemy, she endorses Satan's belief that once the chips are down, God no longer deserves praise. For Job's wife, praise at this point serves no purpose. Job pushes her away, claiming her words to be foolish ranting. "Shall we accept good from God, and not trouble?" (Job 2:10). With this question Job remains anguished but faithful.

Job's wife has been called "Satan's handmaiden" and considered a second Eve. In Genesis, the first book of both the Hebrew and Christian Bible, Eve tempts Adam to go against God's direct order and to eat from a tree in the middle of the Garden of Eden, commonly referred to as the Tree of Knowledge. Once they eat the forbidden fruit from the tree, they are cast out of paradise for committing what is considered the first (or original) sin. In this narrative, Eve is the cause of man's downfall, for she convinces Adam to do what he knows is contradictory to God's will. In another biblical narrative, Sarah encourages her husband, Abraham, to disobey God as well. God makes known to Abraham that he will be the father of many nations. After years of childlessness, Sarah persuades Abraham to take Hagar, their handmaiden, as his concubine. As opposed to remaining faithful to God's plan, Abraham and Hagar produce a son, Ishmael.

Much like the other biblical wives, Job's wife also goes against what she knows is God's will. She works to spread Satan's message of blaspheming God to Job, since Satan cannot do it himself. If Job takes his wife's advice, she will be a widow. Such a status would leave her destitute with little financial support. Pity alone will not convince a wife to take this action with these horrendous repercussions. But as F. Rachel Magdalene of Augustana College argues,

Job's wife is taking pity on herself. She, too, suffers great losses. The narratives do little to describe her anguish other than to cast her as an antagonist and apathetic to her husband's plight. Her response should be criticized with consideration to her feelings about the situation as well. Wiersbe explains, "Rather than watch her husband waste away in pain and shame, she would prefer that God strike him dead and get it over with immediately."

One may wonder why his wife is spared. Job has lost his wealth, his children, and his health. Why has his wife not been taken from him also? A number of things can be read into her survival. First, her sole purpose is to be Satan's mouthpiece. Second, she is a character meant to further the narrative and add another perspective to Job's ordeal. Third, she is a character meant to magnify Job's suffering. If another individual believes the suffering is great enough to curse God, then so, too, should Job.

In Sickness and in Health

While Job's wife is ridiculed in a number of accounts for urging Job to end his suffering by cursing God, thereby facilitating his death, she should also be commended for a number of reasons. Through all of Job's trials, she remains faithful to him. She is by his side through the suffering. She does not receive the same physical pain that Job does, but she does share his emotional suffering. The experience of losing children is shared by Job and his wife. But the narratives do not show her blaming Job for this. She does not castigate him for this. She seeks to put an end to his suffering because she cannot stand to see her husband in agony. So, while many would criticize her as being the "devil's mouthpiece," many would argue that she is instead being a supportive wife.

Magdalene encourages a sympathetic reading of the text with regard to Job's wife, saying:

> Such a reading might begin to try to hear the cry of despair of a woman who has toiled to provide food and a home for her family and who has seen these destroyed. It might begin to articulate the cry of agony of a woman who has labored to give birth to ten children and who has seen them murdered. Such a reading might begin to uncover the cry of pain of a woman who has been a faithful companion to her husband but who is debased by him. It might begin to understand the cry of frustration of a woman who fully understands the intellectual issues involved but who is not taken seriously. Such a reading might begin to feel the cry of rejection of a woman who is made in the image of God but who remains unanswered by God. It might begin to recognize the cry of confusion of a woman who is expected to rebuild her home and to produce more children with no hope of a future for them. Such a reading might begin to speak forth the cry of outrage of a woman who sees her daughters treated in a different way to her sons. Such a reading would begin to embrace this woman's untold story.

The Testament of Job in the Apocrypha also makes Job's wife, named Sitidos, a major player in the story. Sitidos is not the silent sufferer the Bible portrays her to be. With no more riches, she is forced to become a maidservant for other men of the city. The text does not provide information regarding the name of Sitidos's employer. She is concerned with Job's well-being because her food rations have been reduced by half by the unnamed man that she works for in the city. Disguising himself as a bread seller, Satan approaches Sitidos and propositions her to sell her hair in exchange for three loaves of bread for Job. She relinquishes her mane and receives the bread. Upon returning to her husband, she cries out:

> Job! Job! How long wilt thou sit upon the dung-hill outside of the city, pondering yet for a while and expecting to obtain your hoped-for salvation! And I have been wandering from place to place, roaming about as a hired servant, behold thy memory has already died away from earth. And my sons and the daughters that I carried on my bosom and the labors and pains that I sustained have been for nothing? And thou sittest in the malodorous state of soreness and worms, passing the nights in the cold air. (Testament of Job 6: 1–4)

She goes on to say how the public is astonished by the fact that someone with the previous wealth that she had now has to barter for a few loaves of bread. Sitidos instructs Job to eat the bread she brought him, then "curse God and die" (Testament of Job 6:20). Encouraging him further, she acknowledges that if she was in his position, she would give her life to end such suffering. Job understands that Satan must be behind his wife's opinion and says, "Dost thou not see the Seducer stand behind thee and confound thy thoughts in order that thou shouldst beguile me" (Testament of Job 6:23). In the Testament Satan is angered by Job's continued faithfulness and humbles himself before Job. He knows that Job's faithfulness can not be swayed.

The Qur'an gives his wife the name Rahma and gives her a more prominent role in the story. Accordingly, Rahma is approached by Shaitan (Satan) in human form saying he knows a way to cure her husband of his illness. He instructs her to slaughter a sheep in his name instead of the name of Allah; the meat will cure Ayoub. When she goes to Ayoub to tell him of the offer, he asks her about her loyalty to Allah, saying:

> Has the enemy of my Lord misled you? Pity on you! How many years did we enjoy a life of happiness due to the Mercy of Allah? (www.anwary-islam.com)

Rahma answers that they have enjoyed the riches for 80 years. Then Ayoub asks about the length of time that they have been suffering through the trial. She affirms that Ayoub has suffered for seven years. Then he replies:

> Why should we not bear all this for the same period of time as we lived happily? By God! If I am relieved of my afflictions I will flog you with a hundred lashes for your evil suggestion (www.anwary-islam.com).

Job then tells her to go away and leave him alone. In none of the narratives does Job heed his wife's advice. He is firm in his devotion to God.

In an alternate interpretation of this event, Alan Cooper examines the literal translation of Job's wife's speech. Cooper claims that in many biblical texts, Job's wife says, "Bless God and die." Cooper states: "The admonition to 'bless God and die,' in my view, does not advocate blasphemy, nor do I think that the use of 'bless' in that phrase is a euphemistic substitute for 'curse.' 'Bless God and die,' rather is an elliptical way of saying 'petition God for the blessing of death,' which is exactly what Job does." He pleads with an unresponsive God for death.

FALSE COMFORTERS

The term "Job's comforter" has been coined to describe one who intends to convey sympathy to an individual, but in actuality adds to the person's sorrow by claiming that the person brought it upon him- or herself, as Job's friends did. Such an individual offers little help or assistance to the person in need. However, the "comforter" ends up doing more harm than good to the injured party. Undoubtedly, Job is in need of assistance during this time. In his mind, his wife has betrayed him and he is alone. With all the good that he has done in the community and as respected as he is, there is no reason for him to suffer unaided. Soon enough a number of his friends will come to his side to offer support and attempt to arrive at some reasonable cause for Job's predicament.

An indeterminate amount of time passes before Job's three friends, Eliphaz the Temanite, Bildad the Shuhite, and Zophar the Naamathite, arrive to comfort him. It is

Job tormented by demons, by the Flemish master Peter Paul Rubens.

obvious that the men travel a great distance to be by his side during this time of need. When they get there, Job has become so disfigured by his affliction that his friends are unable to recognize him. As they join in his mourning,

58 Job

Job scraping his oozing skin sores with potsherds while surrounded by people. This illustration is from a 12th century manuscript of Moralia in Iob (Morality in Job) *by Pope Gregory the Great.* Moralia in Iob *was one of the most popular works of scriptural interpretation during the Medieval period.*

"they began to weep aloud, and they tore their robes and sprinkled dust on their heads" (Job 2:12). The three men remain silent, as is customary in Hebrew mourning rituals. They are to remain silent until the person enduring the suffering speaks. They sit in silence for seven days and seven nights.

During these days of silence, Job adheres to the second stage of mourning in Hebrew culture. *Shiva* is the Hebrew word for seven, and it refers to the initial week of mourning after burial. During this time the mourner reflects on his or her loss. The mourner sits on a low chair or stool to signify being brought down with grief. Certainly, Job uses this time sitting upon ashes to reflect upon his condition, mourning for the loss of his property, his family, and his health. Lawson comments on the state Job sitting on the heap of ashes declaring, "Under the vicious assaults of the devil, the pained patriarch has sunk into deep despair. Although initially responding with unflinching faith, he begins to weaken under the relentless attack of the devil." But Job can no longer sit silently through the pain.

When Job finally speaks, we hear the words of a very different man. Eaton confirms, "It is as though a saint had suddenly leapt from a stained glass window with rolling eyes and angry words." While he still does not curse God, he does curse the night he was conceived and the day he was born. "May the day of my birth perish. . . . May that night be barren; may no shout of joy be heard in it" (Job 3:3, 7). It would be better if he had never been born than have to endure such agony. Job views death as relief and rest from his endless suffering.

In the midst of this pain-filled existence, Job does not consider taking his own life. The same scrap of pottery that he scratched his sores with could put an end to his life, but he does not consider this. Suicide is comparable to blasphemy; it is not an option for Job. While he does question the Lord's wisdom by asking why he saw fit to create him, Job does not go as far as to take away what the Lord has made. Job realizes that everything he has spent his life avoiding is now happening to him, and he cries out: "What I feared has come upon me; what I dreaded has happened to me. I have no peace, no quietness; I have no rest, but only turmoil" (Job 3:25–26). This statement is a reminder of his earlier actions of sacrificing a burnt offering to the Lord for his children. The biblical text says that this was Job's regular custom. Job safeguards his children against their possible sins. Job is despondent about his situation. It is beyond his understanding as to why he is in this predicament. If God truly loves him, he would not allow him to spend his days suffering. Job desires to move on to Sheol, which he saw as "a shadowy place where the small and great rested together, away from the burdens and sufferings of life on earth." Why does death not come swiftly?

Job, much like his religious brethren, follows a simple dogma: If you believe in God and do his works, you will be rewarded. If you do not, you will be punished. Job is pious, he follows God in every way, and he is rewarded. But that is all gone now. So the question remains, Why do good men suffer? Job ponders this question but does not arrive at a definite conclusion. Attempting to figure out why he is afflicted takes its toll on Job.

> Sheol is a place beneath the earth, considered a grave or a state of death. Many passages in the Bible refer to Sheol. In some cases it is a place of punishment. God can deliver an individual from Sheol.

False Comforters 61

Job grieves with his friends Eliphaz the Temanite, Bildad the Shuhite, and Zophar the Naamathite.

Job is no longer the powerful figure he was before his fall. He is knocked down a peg. He no longer garners the same attention in the town as he did previously. The afflicted Job is alienated from the community he has taken pride in, and he sorrowfully refrains, "And now their sons mock me in song; I have become a byword among them. They detest me and keep their distance; they do not hesitate to spit in my face" (Job 30:9–10). To go from being revered to being spat upon is a mighty blow to one's ego. Job wants nothing more than to plead his case before God and get answers from him regarding why he is being mistreated.

Job and his three friends cannot fathom unwarranted suffering. They follow the doctrine that God punishes the evil and rewards the righteous. By adhering to this strict cause-and-effect relationship, Job's friends are unable to believe anything other than Job's wickedness. He has sinned in some way, and the only way to make things right with God is to repent. Eliphaz, the son of Esau, is the first of the three men to speak, and he bases much of his logic on his own personal experience. Because of these facts and the language of his rhetoric, we can assume Eliphaz to be the eldest of the comforters. His land of origin is Teman. The Bible states:

> Is there no longer wisdom in Teman? Has counsel perished from the prudent? Has their wisdom decayed? (Jeremiah 49:7)

Hailing from a land recognized for its wisdom, Eliphaz undoubtedly believes that he knows the cause of Job's affliction. Eliphaz is sympathetic to Job's plight and asks if he may speak without Job becoming impatient with him. He questions Job: "Consider now: Who, being innocent, has ever perished? Where were the upright destroyed? (Job 4:7). His advice to Job is, "But if it were I, I would appeal to God; I would lay my cause before him" (Job 5:8). He is certain that Job has sinned against God in some way. He speaks of a lion who wails, but his teeth are broken. The lion is unable to find prey, and his cubs are lost to him. In this way, Eliphaz is insinuating that despite his powerful show, Job is irresponsible and unable to care for his family. He goes on to tell of a spirit who came to him in the night and whispered: "Can a mortal be more righteous than God? Can a man be more pure than his Maker?" (Job 4:17). The message behind the dream is that no man, Job included, is perfect before God.

Job responds by claiming that he is under attack. "The

arrows of the Almighty are in me, my spirit drinks in their poison; God's terrors are marshaled against me" (Job 6:4). He feels that he is helpless to free himself from this predicament because he has nothing. He asks his friends to consider his character. Knowing that his integrity is on the line, he assures them that he would not lie to their faces and that he has done nothing wrong. He questions God:

> If I have sinned, what have I done to you, O watcher of men? Why have you made me your target? Have I become a burden to you? Why do you not pardon my offenses and forgive my sins? (Job 7:20–21)

Distraught and miserable, Job can do nothing but question God for the role Job feels he played in his situation. He also believes that he is so far gone that he is near death.

Bildad, Job's second friend to speak, is possibly a descendant of Abraham (through Keturah.) He articulates his opinion of the circumstances, but he does not take up for Job. Instead he asserts God's righteousness, rhetorically asking if God would punish someone unjustifiably: "Surely God does not reject a blameless man or strengthen the hand of evildoers" (Job 8:20). His belief system will not allow him to entertain such a thought. Bildad relies on the wisdom of those elders who came before him and encourages Job to consult them for answers. Lawson writes, "These godly ancestors taught this principle: where there is suffering, it is the result of sin. Such were the traditions of men, and such was the content of Bildad's counsel." He agrees with Eliphaz and tells Job that his hope will perish because he has forgotten God.

Job is rebuked by his friends. This illustration is by the 19th-century French artist Gustave Doré.

Job knows that he cannot argue this with God; he feels he will be unable to prove his innocence, saying, "Indeed, I know that this is true. But how can a mortal be righteous before God?" (Job 9:2). If Job debates with God, he will be considered guilty. He does, however, desire to meet with him and speak his innocence to God's face. He believes God will not listen to him, but if given the chance he would say, "Do not condemn me, but tell me what charges you have against me. Does it please you to oppress me, to spurn the work of your hands, while you smile on the schemes of the wicked?" (Job 10:2–3). What Job is implying is that God delights in witnessing his suffering while allowing evil to reign uncontrollably. Job curses the day he was born, asking why he had even been conceived. It is as if Job believes God has created him for the sole purpose of tormenting him.

Zophar, the third friend, speaks against Job's recriminations. He desires God to speak only to refute Job's misguided beliefs. According to Wiersbe, "He is merciless and tells Job that God was giving him far less than he deserved for his sins!" He reaffirms the fact that God punishes only the wicked: "Surely he recognizes deceitful men; and when he sees evil, does he not take note?" (Job 11:11) Thus, Job must be that evil man. According to their logic there is no way he cannot be guilty. Zophar, whose name means "rough," lives up to that defining characteristic. As Lawson asserts, "Zophar is rude and curt, probably out of growing frustration, as he relies heavily on assumptions. He is the voice of orthodoxy, unbending and pointed in his belief that Job must repent for his sins." Zophar believes Job does not understand the greatness of God, asking if he can fathom the mysteries and limits of God.

While it is obviously exasperating for Job not to be believed by his friends, it must also be frustrating for his friends to see Job and know that his succor can only come from repentance, a thing Job is unwilling to give. He denies the charges against him by Zophar and continues his pleas for a moment with God:

> But I desire to speak to the Almighty and to argue my case with God. You, however, smear me with lies; you are worthless physicians, all of you! If only you would be altogether silent! For you that would be wisdom. (Job 13:3–5)

He no longer needs or wants to hear anything his friends have to say about his affliction. Their presence is not helpful and he can no longer take their ridicule. He tells them to listen to his argument and asks them a number of questions. He asks if they presume to speak for God, if they thought that they could stand in his shoes against God's persecution, and whether they would be terrified if they could not defend themselves.

It seems that Job's comforters are no more than "fair weather friends." Their presence serves only to intensify Job's anger. So harsh is the criticism they level against Job, it is almost unbelievable that they are even his friends in the first place. Lawson responds, "While Job withstood the collapse of his business, the death of his children, and the influence of disease, what came closest to defeating him was the adverse influence of his friends." They cannot understand Job's suffering outside of thinking that he must have brought it upon himself.

In this time of deep sorrow and pain, the three men are useless. They have brought no help or comfort; they are simply an impediment to Job's progress, and they magnify his suffering. They no longer look upon Job as a friend. He is completely foreign to them, and is possibly the embodiment of sin. As the conversation continues, the nature of their friendship before the fall can be questioned. How close is their friendship initially if they cannot for one moment consider Job's position? Never do they back down or acquiesce to the idea that his suffering may actually be unwarranted. They simply do not take his words into account at all.

In the second round of dialogue, Eliphaz the Temanite tells Job to quiet his rants, saying, "Your own mouth condemns you, not mine; your own lips testify against you" (Job 15:6). Eliphaz indicts Job simply because he has tried to plead his innocence. He argues that he is just as wise as the other men, and therefore he knows the ways of God and questions Job's knowledge. Eliphaz instructs Job to

False Comforters 67

A 19th century illustration shows Job responding to the criticisms of his friends. "Job had but one answer to make to [their] questions: man cannot comprehend Divine wisdom, whether it reveal itself in inanimate and brute nature or in relation to human beings," writes Louis Ginzberg in Legends of the Jews.

listen to him because he has seen and heard wise men speak of God's dealings with the wicked. His knowledge base comes from experience; events that he has lived through and seen of the wicked color his viewpoint. Eliphaz says:

> He will no longer be rich and his wealth will not endure, nor will his possessions spread over the land. . . . Let him not deceive himself by trusting what is worthless, for he will get nothing in return. Before his time he will be paid in full, and his branches will not flourish. (Job 15:29, 31–32)

Eliphaz strikes at Job's loss of wealth as an indicator of his wrongdoings and alleges that his payment now comes in the form of his afflictions. Accordingly, he believes that Job is a fool for believing that his riches will protect him from harm. The sinful will receive payment, but they will be compensated by a fruitless existence.

Job calls them all "miserable comforters" and declares that if the tables were turned he would not treat them as they have seen fit to treat him; he would not prosecute them, charging them falsely without supportive evidence. Instead Job declares that he would give them encouragement in their time of need, offering succor during such a traumatic time.

While Job is ignorant of the conversation between God and Satan, it seems as if he somehow understands what has happened. Job ponders:

> God has turned me over to evil men and thrown me into the clutches of the wicked. All was well with me, but he shattered me; he seized me by the neck and crushed me. He has made me his target; his archers surround me. Without pity, he pierces my kidneys and spills my gall on the ground. (Job 16:11–13)

While Job believes God to be apathetic to his pain, there is no evidence in the scripture confirming that God does not feel for Job. However, God cannot rescue him; the wager must be seen through until the end. Though Job is reduced to nothing more than an outcast, he holds strong to the belief that he is righteous and therefore will prosper. But Job's anger is prevalent. He is angered by the realization that those who are unjust continue to thrive in the world, while he is punished beyond measure.

Bildad the Shuhite encourages Job once again to refrain from giving his long speeches. He urges him to be sensible and listen to those who know more than he does concerning these matters. Compounding what Eliphaz has already laid out as the physical repercussions of the wicked, Bildad calls out Job's reputation:

> The memory of him perishes from the earth; he has no name in the land. He is driven from light to darkness and is banished from the world. He has no offspring or descendants among his people, no survivor where he once lived. (Job 18:17–20).

Job cannot understand why his friends continue with their accusations. Even though he knows and states his punishment is unjustified, none of them acknowledge his testimony. None of his friends consider what they know of him from his past actions or his character before he is afflicted. Feeling that he has nothing left, Job continues to mourn for all that he has lost. He laments that he has no kinsmen and no servants. He is offensive to his wife and is hated by his closest friends. He asks the men to have pity on him and not to strike at him as God has done. And while his present predicament is utterly devoid of any comfort, Job holds on to his hope for the future, exclaiming:

> I know that my Redeemer lives and that in the end he will stand upon the earth. And after my skin has been destroyed, yet in my flesh I will see God; I myself will see him with my own eyes—I, and not another. How my heart yearns within me. (Job 19:25–27)

Job calls God his redeemer because he knows that he will one day, even if it is in death, be rescued from his current state. In this testimony we see the true faithfulness of Job.

Job is also a man of integrity. Therefore, he cannot admit to the wrongdoing that his friends accuse him of committing. Nor can he reject the principle that God punishes evildoers. In the biblical book Deuteronomy, after Moses gives the Israelites the Ten Commandments, he goes on to emphasize the importance of being obedient to God: "If you fully obey the Lord your God and carefully follow his commands I give you today, the Lord your God will set you high above all the nations on earth. . . . However, if you do not obey the Lord your God and do not carefully follow all his commands and decrees I am giving you today, all these curses will upon you and overtake you" (Deuteronomy 28:1, 15). Moses then goes into detail regarding curses upon the disobedient falling upon

Job's friends believe that the loss of Job's fortune is a sign that Job's behavior has offended God. "Total darkness lies in wait for his treasures," Zophar says of an unrighteous man. "A fire unfanned will consume him and devour what is left in his tent. The heavens will expose his guilt; the earth will rise up against him. A flood will carry off his house, rushing waters on the day of God's wrath. Such is the fate God allots the wicked, the heritage appointed for them by God" (Job 20:26-29).

his children and animals. There is no doubt that Job and his three friends live by this doctrine. Moses brought these words from God himself. How then can Job's suffering be unwarranted? In the eyes of Eliphaz, Bildad, and Zophar, Job is guilty. For Job, the matter is a mystery. As Green points out, "If he denied the position of his friends, then the plain inference was that God was unjust. If he assented to it, then God was unjust. And, in either case, how could he serve a God who was unjust or cruel?"

Zophar tells Job that he is lying. He reminds Job of how it has been since the beginning of time; the wicked are punished. He strikes at the heart of Job's condemnation, saying:

> He will spit out the riches he swallowed. . . . He will not enjoy the streams, the rivers flowing with honey and cream. . . . Nothing is left for him to devour; his prosperity will not endure. In the midst of his plenty, distress will overtake him; the full force of misery will come upon him. (Job 20:15–22)

Job requests that his friends listen very carefully to him and questions why the truly wicked continue to prosper. Life for evildoers is undisturbed; they are powerful, free of fear, and die peacefully. He knows what their response will be without them having to say anything. Job tells them, "I know full well what you are thinking, the schemes by which you would wrong me. You say, 'Where now is the great man's house, the tents where wicked men lived?'" (Job 21:27–28).

Bildad responds that all men are born sinners. "How then can a man be righteous before God? How can one born of woman be pure?" (Job 25:4). What follows is perhaps the longest oration in the story. Job will not admit that his friends are right; his integrity will not allow him. With reasons unknown to him, God turns his back on him. Job feels he is silent in times of great need and begins to elucidate on the theme of locating wisdom. While man can search the world for riches such as silver, gold, and iron, wisdom cannot be found. Only God knows where wisdom lies.

In this speech Job also reminisces on his more prosperous days. Besides being admired in the community, Job is charitable. He says: "If I have denied the desires of the poor or let the eyes of the widow grow weary, if I have kept my bread to myself, not sharing it with the fatherless—but from my youth I reared him as would a father, and from my birth I guided the widow—if I have seen anyone perishing for lack of clothing, or a needy man without a garment, and his heart did not bless me for warming him with the fleece from my sheep, . . . then these would be my sins to be judged, for I would have been unfaithful to God on high" (Job 31:16–28). Job is good to those in need, using his riches to bless those who are not as fortunate. He has given meat from his own flocks and given lodge to anyone without a place to stay. These are things that everyone in the town knows about Job.

Job is delivering what can be considered akin to an Egyptian death oration. Compiled within the Book of the Dead are volumes of mortuary texts in which Eaton asserts, "the person is imagined as posthumously affirming before a court of gods his innocence of various sins, including adultery, lying, stealing, murder, fraud, mistreatment of animals, and blasphemy. Sometimes there are positive claims: 'I have given bread to the hungry, water to the thirsty, clothing to the naked, and a boat to one who was marooned." Job is confident about the righteousness of what he has done. Nevertheless, Job's friends are not swayed by his emotional testimony. They refused to believe that he has not brought his suffering upon himself.

Among the most jarring moments in the narrative is when, out of nowhere, a fourth man, Elihu, appears and decides to speak. Elihu is the youngest of the visitors and therefore pays respect to his elders by remaining silent until they have finished talking. The narrative introduces Elihu as the son of Barakel the Buzite, from the Ram family. After hearing the preceding discussion, Elihu is angered by Job's fruitless attempts to justify himself to his friends. He is almost arrogant in his claims that just because the others are his elders does not mean they possess more wisdom than him. It is not age, but God, which grants knowledge within an individual. He is attempting to set the stage for his views, and in order to be heard and taken seriously, Elihu states:

> I thought, "Age should speak; advanced years should teach wisdom." But it is the spirit in a man, the breath of the Almighty, that gives him understanding. It is not only the old who are wise, not only the aged who understand what is right." (Job 32:7–9)

Elihu turns to Job and encourages him to listen to him, setting up his speech as if God himself has empowered him to say the following words. Elihu's speech takes a completely divergent view of Job's predicament, expressing a difference in religious doctrine. He misunderstands Job's issue with God, claiming that Job believes himself to be "pure and without sin" (Job 33:9), which is not what Job alleges. According to Elihu, it is God who determines guilt or innocence, and the guilty will be punished in time. He goes on to tell Job that God has not turned his back on him or remained silent to his cries. To the contrary, Job may not have understood God's reply. Green explains Elihu, writing:

> He says that affliction is not a token of God's displeasure but one of the measures of His grace. It is not sent in wrath, but with a kind and merciful design. It is one of the ways in which God draws men from sin and promotes their welfare.

Elihu contends that suffering is not punitive, but practical. Pain is a part of God's plan and program. It does not always indicate his wrath, but his love. Neither Job nor the friends respond to Elihu's contemporary religious dogma. Many critics of the text believe Elihu's speech is added to the text secondarily. His entrance into the text disturbs the narrative flow. It would be logical for God's response to come after Job's speech, not after Elihu's.

In the Testament of Job, his friends provide more comfort to him than in the biblical narrative. After sitting with

The Unknown Comforter

Some Biblical scholars that Elihu's speech was a later addition to the Book of Job. When Job's friends enter the narrative to comfort him, Elihu is the only one not mentioned. Why would he be omitted from this introduction? Later the text indicates that Elihu is the youngest of the friends, and so he waits respectfully until his elders have finished before he chooses to speak. He does not take the same abusive tone with Job as the other men, and in the conclusion he is the only man to escape God's rebuke. Many contend that this is an editorial lapse—Elihu is not mentioned at the end as needing to atone for his sins because he did not appear in the original narrative.

Job for the seven days, they exclaim, "Do we not know how many goods were sent by him to the cities and the villages round about to be given to the poor, aside from all that was given away by him within his own house? How then could he have fallen into such a state of perdition and misery?" (Testament of Job 7:20). Elihu says that they must come closer so that they may see if this person is truly the man they know as Job. It is incomprehensible that someone of his stature has sunk so low that they must carry perfume with them to mask his smell. When they approach, Eliphaz asks if he is in fact the glorious king Job. His next question is whether he is the man that gave 7,000 of his sheep to clothe the poor, 3,000 cattle to plow the field of the poor, and had 60 tables set for the poor. It is important to note that Job is identified not only by his riches, but also by the good he has done with them. His notoriety is determined by his wealth as well as his charity. Eliphaz is quick to quiet his friends from admonishing Job. He declares that they must understand why Job is suffering in this extreme manner. A man of his prominence, who so willingly gives to those in need, is afflicted in such a devastating way that they must obtain an answer. The only possible answer to his suffering has to be his sins.

The Hidden Face of God

Many believers will contend that during times of need, one must pray to God. A belief that God can heal all wounds allows the sufferer some comfort. It would be detrimental to individuals to believe their cries or prayers go unanswered. The only thing that Job knows to do is to plead his case before God. If God hears his cries, he will heal this grievous wrong that is occurring. But through the course of Job's story, his cries seemingly go unanswered.

Job's predicament is not just the fact that he is suffering unjustly, but also that God is ignoring his pleas. During this period Job begs for the opportunity to meet with God so that he may argue his case of innocence. It is Job's belief that the God he serves is just and good; therefore, he has a divine duty to respond to his inquiries. He believes that if he is given this opportunity to speak with God, then all his suffering will be taken away. His wounds will be healed and his health restored. After two of his friends try to reason with him, Job replies:

> How then can I dispute with him? How can I find words to argue with him? Though I were innocent, I could not answer him; I could only plead with my Judge for mercy. Even if I summoned him and he responded, I do not believe that he would give me a hearing. He would crush me with a storm and multiply my wounds for no reason. (Job 9:14–17).

In this rant Job makes a number of things clear. It is obvious he wants the occasion to speak with God, to beg him for forgiveness for offenses he knows he has not done. But he thinks God will not give him a chance to state his claims of innocence. And God will be angered just because Job has called on him, which will cause more agony to befall him. At this point Job feels he has nothing left to lose; he loathes his life and can say whatever he desires. To this end he goes on to maintain that God destroys the blameless and the wicked equally.

This criticism is contrary to the belief his friends argue. In their minds God is not fickle. Job continues his tirade by outright accusing God of enjoying his suffering: "Does it please you to oppress me, to spurn the work of your hands, while you smile on the schemes of the wicked?" (Job 10:2). Job is committing utter blasphemy, but this does not concern him at this point. But just as some narratives tell of Job remaining silent to the question of what should be done about the Israelites, God remains silent to his interrogations. God does not appear to Job.

According to John Calvin, God's refusal to reveal himself to Job "darkens history, threatens faith, and tempts one to despair." However, the very essence of faith

Although Job expresses a desire to look upon the Lord, this may be too much for him to handle. Exodus 33:19 states that no man may see God's face and live. Exodus also describes how Moses is transformed after conversing with a manifestation of God on Mount Sinai. The Bible describes Moses's face as "radiant" (Exodus 34:35) and explains how he put a veil over his face so that he would not frighten the Israelites. Mount Sinai is pictured; at the bottom is Saint Catherine's Monastery, which was built in the sixth century at the place where Moses was believed to have spoken with God.

dictates that it is not necessary for God to show his face for Job to know that he is all-powerful.

Job eventually receives a response to his pleas; God's voice is heard from out of a storm, saying: "Who is this that darkens my counsel with words without knowledge? Brace yourself like a man; I will question you, and you shall answer me" (Job 38:2–3). After his days of supplication, Job assuredly is pleased to have the Lord speak to him. But God does not speak to him in a manner that is to be expected. He does not respond to Job with a statement as to why he has to endure such needless suffering, nor does he let Job in on his earlier conversation with Satan. God's

In the Vulgate, a fifth century translation of the scriptures from Greek and Hebrew into Latin, the Christian priest and scholar Jerome (347-420) read the word qaran *as "horned" (in the scriptures, this word can mean both "horned" and "ray of light," or "radiant.") Thus it became common to depict Moses with horns, such as in this sculpture of the ancient lawgiver by Michelangelo located in Rome's Basilica of St. Peter in Chains.*

response comes in the form of a warning. He cautions Job to prepare himself for a litany of rhetorical questions, which will serve to highlight his sovereign and divine nature. As Green asserts:

> The fact is the Lord's comments were not dedicated to the clearing up of that mystery at all. It is not God's plan to offer a vindication of His dealings with men in general, or a justification of his providence towards Job. He has no intention of placing Himself in a position where His creatures can judge His conduct. He is not amenable to them, and He does not recognize their right to be censors of Him and His ways.

Indeed much of the controversy surrounding the tragedy of Job is that no explanation is ever given. One is left to infer the true meaning behind Job's burden.

By the conclusion of the narrative, answering the question of why innocent people suffer still proves to be an elusive task. Many Hebrews who adhere to the principle of monotheism also understand that if there is one God who is good and just, there is also the presence of evil. According to biblical narratives, pain and suffering entered the world when Adam and Eve were tempted by Satan and disobeyed God's orders. If they had remained faithful to God's law, evil would not exist. But once they defied God and ate from the Tree of Knowledge, they were aware of good and evil, aware of their nakedness, and they were ashamed. For many this momentary indiscretion answers the question as to why good people suffer. So while Job does suffer—unnecessarily to some—it is his inheritance. And therefore he must endure and accept the legacy that is passed down to him. Job and the devoted believers are not to question God's plan or his reasons for life's occurrences; it is as if the simple act of belief should make them immune from the very human need of wanting to know *why*.

The culmination of Job's trials occurs when he is confronted by God. When God questions Job, he makes reference to the leviathan, a symbol of Satan or evil in the world, saying:

> Can you pull in the leviathan with a fishhook or tie down his tongue with a rope? . . . Any hope of subduing him is false; the mere sight of him is overpowering. . . . Behind him he leaves a glistening wake; one would think the deep had white hair. Nothing on earth is his equal—a creature without fear. (Job 41:1, 9, 32–33)

We get an understanding of the true purpose of evil in these lines. They hint at evil being the reason for Job's suffering. But God does not implicitly state this reason. Job utters the words "I know that you can do all things; no plan of yours can be thwarted" (Job 42:2) as proof that God can do anything, including defeating evil. The story is as much about God as it is about Job. As Lawson maintains,

> God controls Satan's power and man's circumstances. The book [of Job] ends with God querying Job about the nature of his own right to rule his creation. This is the primary lesson learned by Job as taught in [the] book. God is God. He will do as he pleases, when he pleases, with whom he pleases, without consulting his creatures, and he will do so for his own glory and the ultimate good of his people.

By reintroducing the image of the leviathan into the conclusion of the narrative, we see that Job's plight comes

"Then the Lord answered Job out of the storm. He said: 'Who is this that darkens my counsel with words without knowledge?' Brace yourself like a man; I will question you, and you shall answer me" (Job 38:1-3)

full circle. Neither Job nor any man can subdue the great sea creature. By setting up the terrible, unconquerable image of the creature, God illustrates his power because only he can control the beast. In God's whirlwind speech he is querying Job: If he cannot control the creature how then can he expect to control God? This speech puts Job and Satan on notice: God is in charge.

God's appearance to Job, in voice alone and through the wind, is a demonstration of his divinity and infinite power. At this point Job is burdened unimaginably, and to some readers this scene plays out like a confrontation. Unlike previously, when Job could counter the arguments of his friends, he is silent before the might of God. As Lawson contends:

> But when Job got what he wanted—a day in court with God—he did not want what he got. God suddenly burst on the scene and spoke to Job out of a whirlwind, asking him over seventy questions. What follows is the longest conversation in the Bible in which God speaks.

Instead of Job questioning God, as he ranted about earlier in the narrative, it is God who questions him. Instead of answering the many claims leveled against him by Job, God decides to respond in the form of questions in order to demonstrate the ridiculousness of Job's queries. "Will the one who contends with the Almighty correct him? Let him who accuses God answer Him!" (Job 40:2). Of course Job does not have the answers to any of God's questions, because Job is not the sovereign Lord. Perhaps the most indicting question comes halfway through the Lord's speech, when he inquires, "Would you discredit my justice? Would you condemn me to justify yourself?" (Job 40:8). In this question we see the major sin that is committed on Job's part.

Susan E. Schreiner compares the viewpoints of Calvin and Aquinas on this issue: "For Aquinas, although Job did not intend to charge God with iniquity, Job's words 'seemed reprehensible.' For Calvin, however, this verse was central and demonstrated that the whirlwind speech finally addressed the overriding problem of Job's self-justification." In order for Job to consistently maintain his innocence, he necessarily indicts God. If he is innocent of all charges, then God is guilty and is unjust in his punishment. This is most certainly not Job's intent; he acknowledges his wrongdoing, saying that he has spoken of things of which he does not have knowledge. Job is humbled, and he repents of his sins. Lawson states, "Job saw God as sovereign Creator of heaven and earth. With a new awareness beyond his previous understanding, he realized that God was greater than all his trials. God was above and beyond his ability to grasp or understand."

In the end Job's trial becomes a pedagogical tool; he learns more about God than he previously knew. According to Cynthia Ozick, "Suffering educates and purifies; it humbles pride, tames the rebel, corrects the scoffer." Job is humbled by God's words and is able to comprehend God's omnipotence in a way he could not before. And while earlier testimony proves that Job is a pious individual who delightfully gives of his riches, it is also apparent that Job enjoys the attention that it bestows upon him. Job mistakenly believes that he is above all. It is possibly this hubris that allows him to believe that he can question God.

In the end Job is able to see the confirmation of his words and his spirit. A pridefulness that was unknown to him is unveiled as the narrative progresses. Much like Isaiah, who is unable to see his own sinfulness until he encounters God, Job is unable to see his prideful nature until God reveals it to him. Isaiah is in mourning for his friend, King Uzziah, and while praying to God to receive a vision, his need for spiritual cleansing is revealed to him. God sends a seraph with a hot coal in his hand to touch to Isaiah's lips, saying, "See, this has touched your lips; your guilt is taken away and your sin is atoned for" (Isaiah 6:6). Job receives a type of burning coal on his lips when God chastises him by answering his cries with questions of his majesty. Job mistakenly believes that God does not concern himself with the daily activities of man. How can he be knowledgeable of his suffering and let it continue? He concludes that what happens to man is a matter of astronomy and nature; what happens to man occurs outside the view of God. Because of this belief, he is fated to suffer. His friend Elihu attempts to discourage this thinking, attesting that God controls everything and is just and merciful.

Job lives another 140 years after his affliction. These remaining years are undoubtedly more rewarding than the years before his trials. According to the epilogue of the biblical narrative, God tells Job's friends how he is

Job repents in the presence of his four friends, and is subsequently blessed by God. This Florentine painting dates from the late 15th century.

angered by their inaccurate statements about him. He instructs them to make a burnt offering of seven bulls and seven rams for themselves while Job prays for them. Job is then blessed again with riches beyond measure:

> The Lord blessed the latter part of Job's life more than the first. He had fourteen thousand sheep, six thousand camels, a thousand yoke of oxen and a thousand donkeys. And he also had seven sons and three daughters. (Job 42:12–13)

The Origins of Sin

Original sin, also known as ancestral sin, occurs in Christian theology when Adam and Eve disobey God's instruction and eat fruit from the forbidden tree. The book of Genesis relates the story of their fall from grace and punishment for eating from the tree of knowledge. Adam and Eve were expelled from the Garden of Eden and Eve cursed to painful childbirth and Adam to painful work. Christians believe that because of this event, sin entered the world; everyone born comes into the world as a sinner.

Schreiner explains Calvin's opinion concerning how the remainder of Job's story plays out, clarifying that "the 'history' of Job's suffering and restoration was written for 'our' benefit in order to show that adversities are temporal and that God will not tempt us more than we can bear. He goes so far as to claim that Job's restoration demonstrates that the 'issue' or 'result' of suffering will be a happy one." Calvin does go back and corrects this statement, saying that God does not always double his blessings.

The Testament of Job provides further information about Job's life after he regains his health:

> And now, my children, let me admonish you: "Behold I die. You will take my place. Only do not forsake the Lord. Be charitable towards the poor; do not disregard the feeble. Take not unto yourselves wives from strangers. Behold, my children, I shall divide among you what I possess, so that each may have control over his own and have full power to do good with his share." (Testament of Job 11:5–7).

It is evident that Job wishes his children to have the same spirit of benevolence that he has. He wants them to give charitably of their riches. Job is instilling in them the need to be compassionate and the necessity of possessing a giving heart. But he redistributes his wealth to his sons only. It seems rather self-centered that immediately after Job details the need for a giving spirit, his three daughters question him about their share of the wealth. Job tells them not to worry, because they have not been forgotten. He has something of greater value to bestow upon them. He instructs one of his daughters to go to the treasure house and bring back a certain golden casket. When she returns with the requested item, Job opens it and gives each daughter a string. He tells them to lace it around them and "all the days of your life they may encircle you and endow you with every thing good" (Testament of Job 11:14). A second daughter, Kassiah, is understandably confused by this offering and questions it, alleging that they cannot live on this piece of thread. But Job tells them:

> Not only have you here sufficient to live on, but these bring you into a better world to live in, in the heavens. Or do you not know my children, the value of these things here? Hear then! When the Lord had deemed me worthy to have compassion on me and to take off my body the plagues and the worms, He called me and handed to me these three strings. And He said to me: "Rise and gird up thy loins like a man I will demand of thee and declare thou unto me." And I took them and girt them around my loins, and immediately did the worms leave my body, and likewise did the plagues and my whole body took new strength through the Lord, and thus I passed on, as though I had never suffered. But also in my heart I forgot the pains. Then spoke the Lord unto me in His great power and showed to me all that was and will be. (Testament of Job 11:16–20)

Job gives them something more valuable than all the riches in the world; he gives them a token proving that all can be endured. He tells them that as long as they have these threads, no evil can befall them. One at a time the three young women girdle themselves, and instantly their hearts are transformed. They no longer have a desire for riches or worldly things. Shortly after he finishes telling the story of his life, Job becomes ill. This time, however, his illness is free of pain or suffering. After a few days he passes away and is mourned by a great many people.

Depending on which narrative you chose to believe, Job is either sentenced unfairly or punished for a past sin of silence. But as pastor John MacArthur points out, suffering may occur for various reasons:

> The major reality of the book is the inscrutable mystery of innocent suffering. God ordains that His children walk in sorrow and pain, sometimes because of sin, sometimes for chastening, sometimes for strengthening, and sometimes to give opportunity to reveal His comfort and grace. But there are times when the compelling issue in the suffering of the saints is unknowable because it is for a heavenly purpose that those on earth can't discern.

And while Job cries out in confusion and his friends posit their theories, no answer as to why the innocent suffer is arrived at by the conclusion of the narrative.

Job in Literature

Other than the story of Moses, the Joban narrative has received more literary adaptations, artistic renderings, and critical analysis than any biblical narrative. Storytellers gravitate to the theme of unjust suffering. This is perhaps the most universal theme because it speaks to people on an emotional level. Regardless of culture, religion, or gender, every person will undergo some type of misery in the course of his or her lifetime. Modern adaptations and critical commentary attempt to make sense of the plight of one good, patient man. His undue suffering causes many modern interpreters to have a negative view of the subject. They fail to see any value in Job's trial. As Schreiner points out: "No contemporary interpreter finds in Job any message of detached transcendence or any belief in the beneficial and curative power of suffering. The modern Job did not embrace his adversities or turn inward to ascend toward God." For modern readings it is not enough to claim that Job gains insight and an understanding of God that he previously lacked. Many interpretations and commentaries are searching for something greater than increased knowledge or awareness. The modern stories discussed in this chapter deal with the major themes of Job's story, including the patience of Job, unjust suffering, and God's punishment of the wicked.

While the Arthurian legends do not specifically speak of Job, the stories possess a religious overtone that was prevalent during the medieval period. The legends focus on some of the key features that arise in the story of Job. Ideas of righteousness, morality, and duty occur throughout the tales of Arthur and the knights of the Round Table. In one particular story, the idea of unjust suffering arises. Sir Lionel is positioned to slay his own brother when a hermit and another knight come to the aid of Sir Lionel's brother. Instead of charging at his sibling, Sir Lionel turns his murderous rage upon the two rescuers and kills them. Later, while relating the story to King Arthur and Queen Guinevere, he is puzzled by the outcome of the exchange and asks Arthur why God did not save them, as they were innocent men who came to the aid of someone in need. Guinevere responds to his question, saying:

> We don't know what their past history was. The killing didn't do harm to their souls. Perhaps it even helped their souls, to die like that. Perhaps God gave them this good death because it was the best thing for them.

In this epic story the idea of human suffering is attributed to past wrongs. The men are being righteous by attempting to save the life of another, but the question arises: What did they do in the past that allowed God to accept and sanction their senseless slaughter? This event

This 14th century tapestry depicts Britain's legendary King Arthur and members of his court. The Arthurian legends are among numerous literary works throughout history that have drawn on the story of Job for inspiration in attempting to explain the causes of human suffering.

The French poet and novelist Victor Hugo, author of such works as Les Misérables, *once commented on the importance of the Book of Job, writing, "Tomorrow, if all literature was to be destroyed and it was left to me to retain one work only, I should save Job."*

is in line with the dominant belief of Job's friends that God only punishes those who commit some offense, thereby making them deserving of punishment. According to the queen, perhaps death is the best thing for those who commit a past transgression.

Past transgressions or lack of devotion to God bringing pain to an individual are issues that are developed in a number of writings. The French author Albert Camus takes up the theme of suffering for past sins in his 1947 novel, *La Peste (The Plague)*. The novel tells the story of a town that is suffering from the plague. Paneloux, the main character, believes that the townspeople are being punished due to their "neglect of God and their duties to the Church." The sin of the townspeople is depicted as equal to the sin of Job. Contrary to the biblical narrative, which does not pointedly indict Job—his friends do that—Camus' character subverts the story so that Job is no longer viewed as the unwitting victim, but rather considered the villain. In the novel the plague becomes a manifestation of the sin committed by the townspeople.

While not the antagonist in his narrative, Job is punished as such. His plague-like symptoms cause him to long for death. He curses the day of his birth as well as the sea, saying, "May those who curse days [or the sea] curse that day, those who are ready to rouse the Leviathan" (Job 3:8). The sea and the creature within it are the subject of Herman Melville's epic novel, *Moby-Dick*. Captain Ahab is searching for the great whale, a creature he calls a leviathan on several occasions. For Ahab, the ever elusive whale is his adversary. Having lost his leg to the creature, he commits himself to revenge, saying, "It was Moby Dick that dismasted me; Moby Dick that brought me to this dead stump I stand on now. Aye, aye . . . it was that accursed white whale that razed me; made a poor pegging lubber of me for ever and a day."

The whale is most certainly unattainable, but Ahab believes it to be his destiny to rid the world of the evil whale and talks the crew into assisting him in this endeavor. He is relentless in his quest. Melville writes, "Ahab had cherished a wild vindictiveness against the whale, all the more fell for that in his frantic morbidness he at least came to identify with him, not only all his bodily woes, but all his intellectual and spiritual exasperations." Everything that is wrong in his world is attributed to the whale, and the only way to remedy the ills Ahab faces is to find and kill Moby Dick.

The narrator of the story, Ishmael, is a junior member of the crew and is an intellectual young man attempting to lose himself at sea. As an educated individual he makes it a point to learn what he can about the great whale. His knowledge base is massive as he counts facts regarding subjects such as phrenology, art, and taxonomy. But he does not understand the motivations of the whale. The great white whale can allegorically symbolize an unknowable God. If the whale symbolizes God, then Ahab symbolizes Job. As author Bert Bender asserts, "Like the unrepentant Job, whose story bears an enormous influence on *Moby-Dick*, Ahab would 'desire to reason with God.' And like the unrepentant Job who spoke 'without knowledge and his words were without wisdom,' Ahab fails to see that 'we cannot order our speech by reason of darkness.'"

The story of Job is structured in such a way that it reads more like a play than a historical account of an individual's life. Excluding the prologue and epilogue, the majority of the story is told through dialogue. The story lends itself to a modern-day drama so much that it should not be surprising that the story of Job has been translated into contemporary stage plays. As Cynthia Ozick asserts:

> His story, because it is mostly in dialogue, reads as a kind of drama. There is no proscenium; there is no scenery. But there is a dazzling spiral of words—extraordinary words, Shakespearean words; and there are six players, who alternately cajole, console, contradict, contend, satirize, fulminate, remonstrate, accuse, deny, trumpet, succumb. . . . The subject is innocence and power; virtue and injustice; the Creator and His creation; or what philosophy has long designated as theodicy, the Problem of Evil.

Archibald MacLeish was awarded the 1959 Pulitzer Prize for his drama *J.B.: A Play in Verse*. A modern

Job speaks with his friends at the height of his distress. This Florentine painting dates from the late 15th century.

retelling of the book of Job, the play is set in the 1950s. The protagonist, J.B., is a successful businessman. He is thankful to God for all the blessings he receives, wealth and a wonderful family. Shortly after the Thanksgiving holiday, tragedy begins to strike at him as his children endure a series of separate accidents until they all die. His wife leaves him, and he becomes painfully ill. All the while he remains faithful to God. MacLeish is consistent with the biblical narrative in telling of the undue affliction of the Joban character; however, many of his arguments differ from the biblical text. According to Schreiner:

> J.B. defends the notion of retributive justice as long as he can, even to the extent of confessing sins he did not commit. J.B. insists that "[God] knows the guilt is mine. He must know: / Has He not punished it? He knows its / Name, its time, its face, its circumstance."

Even if the crime is unknown to him, it must have occurred for him to be experiencing such suffering. That alone is enough to make J.B. confess. The difference between the drama and the biblical text arises in the discussion between J.B. and his wife, Sarah. While J.B. feels that he must confess his mysterious sin, according to Schreiner: "Sarah will have none of J.B.'s guilt. Referring to her children she cries, 'They are / Dead and they were innocent: I will not / Let you sacrifice their deaths / To make injustice justice and God good!" In MacLeish's drama we see what many scholars attempt to understand—the purpose of human suffering. Why must we endure such horrible circumstances in our lives? Such events cannot take place without there being a significant meaning to their occurrences.

In Muriel Spark's 1985 novel *The Only Problem*, we encounter not only the question of suffering, but also issues regarding the methods in which individual pain and distress are handled. The protagonist, Harvey Gotham, is a Canadian millionaire obsessed with writing a treatise about the book of Job and how the question of suffering is treated within the narrative. As Harvey begins the book, he has not undergone any physical suffering, so that his writing is purely an abstraction. However, as the novel progresses, Harvey is caught in a number of events that force him to face the issues he is writing about in his treatise. Harvey concludes, "The only problem in terms of philosophy and religion is the difficulty of facing a benevolent creator who can condone the sufferings of the world." There is no cause or reason except the one that God deems fit, and therein lays the problem. An overwhelming number of people endure suffering without an explicit reason or explanation, and they are powerless to prevent it.

While the story of Job continues to pique the modern imagination, some of the themes dealt with in the narrative predate the biblical telling of his story. The story of Prometheus in Greek mythology has also been compared to Job's life. Most notably told in the epic poet, Hesiod's *Theogony*, Prometheus is a Titan god, credited with creating man. He and Zeus were determining forms of animal sacrifices for man to bestow upon the gods. In an effort to assist man, Prometheus divides the animal parts into two portions. One portion is ox meat and inners wrapped inside the animal's stomach lining. The other packet holds ox bones, but Prometheus covers it in animal fat. Unknowingly, Zeus selects the bones wrapped in fat as offering, while the humans will be able to keep the meat. After being tricked into selecting a less desirable sacrifice,

> The "patience of Job" refers to one who endures long suffering without complaint. "Job's post" refers to a person who brings bad news, much like the servants who come to tell Job of the incidents that cause him to lose his riches, servants, and children.

Zeus withholds fire from man as punishment. In an effort to ensure mankind has access to this necessary element, Prometheus goes to Mount Olympus and steals it from the angered god. Once Zeus finds out about the theft he punishes Prometheus' actions by chaining him to a rock in the Caucasian Mountains for the remainder of his life.

Job is unlike Prometheus in character. He is not a trickster, as Prometheus is, and in most narratives Job does nothing overt to cause his suffering as Prometheus. However, the similarity between the two is identified in their suffering and their methods of dealing with the suffering. Job laments his punishment, crying out for a moment with God so that he may hear his pleas and give

Like the story of Job, the ancient Greek myth of Prometheus also deals with themes of sin and punishment. Unlike Job, however, Prometheus explicitly violates the commandments of the Greek pantheon's ruling deity, Zeus. Prometheus is condemned to be chained to a rock and to have his liver torn out by a large eagle. The Titan's organ regenerates, allowing this punishment to continue, day after day.

audience to his concerns. Prometheus cries out to nature and sings to the gods his objections to his life sentence. While the Titan is bound to the rock, an eagle comes to eat his liver, which regenerates daily. The eagle eating from his body is much like the worms that eat from Job. Prometheus' life is controlled by the gods. He is powerless to stop his torture. He, like Job, is at the whim of another more superior being. Finally, after thousands of years of torture, Heracles comes and kills the eagle, then frees Prometheus from his chains.

The story of Job has in many ways become just as much a myth as that of Prometheus. As Jeff Makos explains in his review of Susan E. Schreiner's text on Job, he has become a mythic hero and a symbol to be interpreted by people at various times to serve their purposes, from early interpretations by Gregory the Great, who uses the story to show "the moral and spiritual progress of the sufferer who strives for purification," to Robert Frost, who uses the character of Job in his 1945 comedic play *A Masque of Reason*. Job's story is accessible and his plight is universal. Sympathizing with a man who suffers as greatly as Job does is something that is not difficult for readers.

But sympathy is not the reason that this story has survived as long as it has or the reason for the frequent allusions to it. Job's story stands the test of time because it is an enigma. The daunting task of grappling with the reasons of unjust suffering is what makes Job's tale everlasting. As Warren W. Wiersbe points out, "But the fundamental reason for Job's suffering was to silence the blasphemous accusations of Satan and prove that a man would honor God even though he has lost everything." In this way we see that it is not Job who is on trial, as many critics assert. The person on trial is, in fact, God. Job is a witness; he is a character witness meant to provide a living testimony of the undeniable reputation of God. He is meant to prove that no matter the situation, God is worthy of and will receive praise.

But through reading the story, one comes to understand that it is not so much a tale about undue suffering or why the just are focused in the crosshairs of evil. Job's story is also about a man who attempts to understand the will of God. As Wiersbe points out: "Theology is a necessary science, but it is also a difficult science; for it is our attempt to know the Unknowable. God has revealed himself in creation, in province, in His Word, and supremely in His Son; but our understanding of what God has revealed may not always be clear." By the conclusion of the story, Job still does not understand why he is tested. But he learns, in essence, not to ask.

According to Maimonides, the story of Job demonstrates the goal of human existence, which is knowledge of God. Once Job is knowledgeable concerning God's providence, as Cooper agrees, he "ceases to be troubled by the loss of his health, wealth, and children—things that he had only 'imagined' to be sources of happiness—and experiences 'true happiness, which is knowledge of the deity.'" Understanding of a higher power or the presence of someone greater than oneself leads to a sense of ultimate security. The insignificant things in life are no longer a pressing concern. That explanation may not suffice for some who believe that while the riches Job lost are most definitely replaceable, his children cannot be substituted. His days and nights in agonizing pain cannot be erased, and his loved ones cannot be returned. As Lawson states, "More importantly the anguish he experience[d] is used by God to show the sovereign workings of God behind the veiled curtain of human circumstances for his own glory."

Job in Literature

The curtain is never truly lifted for Job. He still remains in the dark about the conversation with Satan. He is not privy to the fact that his burden all began with a wager between creature and Creator, with him as the pawn. However, this knowledge of a divine being brings comfort to faithful believers such as Job. God is no longer the cloaked individual that Job has heard stories about and blindly burned offerings to because he thinks it is the appropriate thing to do. He now has a relationship with God. And while he does not have the knowledge of the inner workings of God's holy plan, it is acceptable to him. Job does not need to know of Satan's proposition to recognize the presence of God and his sovereignty.

In the end, trauma is the vehicle that allows for Job's realization. There is an unyielding belief that springs from

Changing the Question

Many times in the midst of a tragedy, people are likely to ponder the question *why*. Why must the innocent suffer, why does this happen? Questions of this nature generally leave the petitioner with little succor. Job's rants culminate in a divine monologue from God. No clear answers are given for the reason people suffer. Job is gratified by what he comes away with after God's speech. However, what may prove to be more comforting is to take the route that Job, in the midst of his suffering, cannot—trying to understand what can be taken away or learned from the situation. The questioning gave Job little peace. Once he abandons his infuriated inquiry into his situation, he is able to witness fully the glory of God. He learns more than he could have imagined. At the end of his life, he is a richer man for having endured the trials. He is able to live out the remainder of his days in peace, satisfied with his life.

The theophany of Job, as described in Job 38-42. A theophany is a manifestation of God in the Bible that is tangible to the human senses. In this late 18th century Italian painting, the Lord is depicted as the pre-incarnate Jesus Christ.

experiencing a traumatic event such as Job has gone through. While the affliction sent down from Satan ravages his body for a time, he made it to the other side of the pain. In Job's story one can see that trauma allows for individual testimony, not only Job's but also the testimony of his friends, to be heard and witnessed by others. It allows for a clearer understanding of oneself and the knowledge of the necessary presence of God in one's life. Through experiencing a range of traumatic events, the eradication of his flocks and land, the devastation of his wealth, and the untimely death of his children, Job is finally able to understand the meaning behind his daily offering. It is no longer a routine done for his children out of fear in the attempt to stave off an angry retributive God. It is now a task he willingly carries out that necessitates his praise and thanksgiving to God for opening the eyes of a one-time arrogantly wealthy individual.

In the end we see that Job's wealth is not enough; he cannot buy his way out of his dire circumstances. He cannot pay one of his lowly servants or one of the needy that he aided to take his place on the ash heap. He came to realize that his generosity means nothing if it is done pridefully. Job has to realize that everything he has is nothing unless he has a true knowledge of God. In the conclusion, Job "comes forth as gold," for he is rich beyond measure, and not by the doubling of his previous fortune or by the restoration of his family. Job lives out the remainder of his life with a wealth he has not known before his fall. He is rich in understanding and rich in his will to serve God.

Notes

CHAPTER ONE: OVERVIEW

p. 11: "Job belongs to the West…" Susan E. Schreiner, *Where Shall Wisdom Be Found?* (Chicago: University of Chicago Press, 1994), p. 1.

p. 12: "Here is the inspired record…" Steven J. Lawson, *Holman Old Testament Commentary: Job* (Nashville: Broadman & Holman, 2004), p. 2.

p. 13: "If so this would make…" Lawson, *Holman Old Testament Commentary: Job*, 6.

p. 14: "[Some scholars advance] Solomon…" Lawson, *Holman Old Testament Commentary: Job*, 6.

p. 14: "the day of kings, around…" Lawson, *Holman Old Testament Commentary: Job*, 6.

p. 14: "the Joban legend passed through…" Quoted in Schreiner, *Where Shall Wisdom Be Found?*, 157.

p. 14: "Part folk tale, part epic…" Thomas G. Long, *Theology Today* (Princeton: Theological Seminary), www.theologytoday.ptsem.edu.

p. 17: "Moses may have been God's…" Jonathan Kirsch, *Moses: A Life* (New York: Ballantine, 1998), p. 130.

p. 18: "God is seen reigning sovereignly…" Lawson, *Holman Old Testament Commentary: Job*, 11.

p. 19: "'a parable intended to set…" Alan Cooper, *The Sense of the Book of Job* (Baltimore, MD: Johns Hopkins University Press, 1997), p. 228.

p. 19: "intended to set forth the..." Schreiner, *Where Shall Wisdom Be Found?* 61.

p. 20: "Wisdom is hidden from humans..." Quoted in Cooper, *The Sense of the Book of Job*, 235.

p. 21: "a world ruled by a God..." J. H. Eaton, *Job* (London: T&T Clark International, 1985), p. 2.

p. 21: "The Prologue and Epilogue remind..." Eaton, *Job*, 31.

p. 22: "the case of piety..." William Henry Green, *The Book of Job Unfolded* (Arlington Heights: Christian Liberty, 1996), 120.

CHAPTER TWO: JOB'S LIFE AND STATUS

p. 26: "We read of the land..." John Gill, "The New John Gill Exposition of the Entire Bible" (www.studylight.org/com/geb/view.cgi?book=job&chapter=001&verse=001).

p. 26: "wealth [is] measured primarily..." Warren W. Wiersbe, *Be Patient: Waiting on God in Difficult Times* (Colorado Springs: Cook Communications Ministries, 2004), p. 14.

p. 30: "weighed against a 'sucking lamb...'" Kirsch, *Moses: A Life*, 49.

p. 30: "He helped support every good..." Eli Teitelbaum, *And Iyov Was Silent*. http://www.campsci.com/hagadah/and_iyov_was_silent.htm

p. 31: "Like Paul Bunyan, Job is..." Long, *Theology Today*. www.theologytoday.ptsem.edu

p. 31: "The transformation of Job..." Cooper, *The Sense of the Book of Job*, 231.

p. 32: ""To punish Pharaoh . . ." Louis Ginzberg, *Legends of the Jews* vol. 1. Trans. Henrietta Szold and Paul Radin. (Philadelphia: The Jewish Publication Society, 2003), 497.

p. 33: "Because [Job] is unidentified..." Cynthia Ozick, "The Impious Impatience of Job" *American Scholar* 67, no. 4 (Autumn 1998), 15

CHAPTER THREE: MUCH IS TESTED

p. 35: "There is a superior restraint..." Green, *The Book of Job Unfolded*, 14.

p. 37: "Job was deeply rooted in..." Lawson, *Holman Old Testament Commentary: Job*, 13.

p. 38 "For whomever the Lord..." Quoted in Schreiner, *Where Shall Wisdom Be Found?* 95.

p. 38: "preeminent proof that God afflicts..." Quoted in Schreiner, *Where Shall Wisdom Be Found?* 96.

p. 39: "a refined form of ..." Green, *The Book of Job Unfolded*, 25.

p. 39: "The only reason Job fears..." Wiersbe, *Be Patient: Waiting on God in Difficult Times*, 16.

p. 39: "whether there is such a..." Green, *The Book of Job Unfolded*, 26.

p. 40: "a scene of high..." Long, *Theology Today*. www.theologytoday.ptsem.edu

p. 40: "From the first chapter of..." Quoted in Schreiner, *Where Shall Wisdom Be Found?*, 92–93.

p. 40: "Therefore, although the biblical..." Schreiner, *Where Shall Wisdom Be Found?*, 93.

p. 41: "Now Satan betook himself . . ." Ginzberg, *Legends of the Jews*, 456.

p. 41: "So callous does God..." Cooper, *The Sense of the Book of Job*, 230.

CHAPTER FOUR: MOURNING SONG

p. 44: "In the account of the messengers..." Eaton, *Job*, 2.

p. 45: "The tearing of the garments..." David Abelman, *Jewish Guide to Mourning*, www.jewishmag.com.

p. 48: "There the city garbage was deposited..." Wiersbe, *Be Patient: Waiting on God in Difficult Times*, 19.

p. 49: "to see the world's evil..." Eaton, *Job*, ix.

p. 52: "Rather than watch her husband..." Wiersbe, *Be Patient: Waiting on God in Difficult Times*, 20.

p. 53: "Such a reading might begin..." Magdalene, "Job's Wife as

Hero: A Feminist-forensic Reading of the Book of Job."
Biblical Interpretation 14, no. 3 (2006), 209.

p. 55: "The admonition to 'bless God'..." Cooper, *The Sense of the Book of Job*, 233.

CHAPTER FIVE: FALSE COMFORTERS

p. 59: "Under the vicious assaults..." Lawson, *Holman Old Testament Commentary: Job*, 34.

p. 59: "It is as though a..." Eaton, *Job*, 3.

p. 60: "a shadowy place where..." Wiersbe, *Be Patient: Waiting on God in Difficult Times*, 23.

p. 63: "These godly ancestors..." Lawson, *Holman Old Testament Commentary: Job*, 77.

p. 65: "He is merciless..." Wiersbe, *Be Patient: Waiting on God in Difficult Times*, 24.

p. 65: "Zophar is rude and curt..." Lawson, *Holman Old Testament Commentary: Job*, 9.

p. 66: "While Job withstood..." Lawson, *Holman Old Testament Commentary: Job*, 43.

p. 67: "Job had but one answer . . ." Ginzberg, *Legends of the Jews*, 459.

p. 71: "If he denied the position..." Green, *The Book of Job Unfolded*, 81.

p. 72: "the person is imagined..." Eaton, *Job*, 56.

p. 74: "He says that affliction..." Green, *The Book of Job Unfolded*, 95.

CHAPTER SIX: THE HIDDEN FACE OF GOD

p. 77: "darkens history, threatens faith..." Quoted in Schreiner, *Where Shall Wisdom Be Found?*, 94.

p. 80: "The fact is the Lord's..." Green, *The Book of Job Unfolded*, 101.

p. 81: "God controls Satan's power..." Lawson, *Holman Old Testament Commentary: Job*, 7–8.

p. 83: "But when Job got what..." Lawson, *Holman Old Testament Commentary: Job*, 326.

p. 83: "For Aquinas, although Job..." Schreiner, *Where Shall Wisdom Be Found?*, 139.

p. 84: "Job saw God as sovereign..." Lawson, *Holman Old Testament Commentary: Job*, 364.

p. 84: "Suffering educates and purifies..." Ozick, "The Impious Impatience of Job," 15.

p. 87: "the 'history' of Job's..." Schreiner, *Where Shall Wisdom Be Found?*, 148.

p. 89: "The major reality..." MacArthur, 694.

CHAPTER SEVEN: JOB IN LITERATURE

p. 90: "No contemporary interpreter..." Schreiner, *Where Shall Wisdom Be Found?*, 158.

p. 91: "We don't know what..." T. H. White, *Once and Future King* (New York: ACE, 1987), p. 449.

p. 92: "neglect of God and their..." Andrea Lesic-Thomas, "The Answer Job Did Not Give: Dostoevsky's Brat'ia Karamazovy and Camus's La Peste" *Modern Language Review* (2006), 777

p. 93: "It was Moby Dick..." Herman Melville, *Moby-Dick* (New York: Bantam, 1967), p. 156.

p. 93: "Ahab had cherished a wild..." Melville, *Moby-Dick*, 175.

p. 94: "Like the unrepentant Job..." Bert Bender, "*Moby Dick*, an American Lyrical Novel," in *Studies in the Novel* 10, no. 3 (1978), 97.

p. 94: "His story, because it is..." Ozick, "The Impious Impatience of Job," 15.

p. 96: "J.B. defends the notion..." Schreiner, *Where Shall Wisdom Be Found?*, 174.

p. 96: " Sarah will have none..." Schreiner, *Where Shall Wisdom Be Found?*, 174.

p. 97: "The only problem in terms..." Angela Hague, "The Only Problem" *Magill's Literary Annual*, (G.P. Putnam's Sons, 1985), 179.

p. 99: "the moral and spiritual progress..." Jeff Makos, *Job's Story: Centuries of Analysis*.
http://chronicle.uchicago.edu/940929/schreiner.shtml

p. 99: "But the fundamental reason..." Wiersbe, *Be Patient: Waiting on God in Difficult Times*, 16.

p. 100: "Theology is a necessary science..." Wiersbe, *Be Patient: Waiting on God in Difficult Times*, 131.

p. 100: "ceases to be troubled..." Cooper, *The Sense of the Book of Job*, 229.

p. 100: "More importantly the anguish..." Lawson, *Holman Old Testament Commentary: Job*, 11.

Glossary

Apocrypha—a term coined by the fifth-century biblical scholar Saint Jerome that refers to the biblical books included as part of the Septuagint (the Greek version of the Old Testament) but not included in the Hebrew Bible. These same books are referred to by Protestants as the pseudepigrapha.

blasphemy—Using the name of the Lord in a vulgar, idle, or trifling manner; use of God's name in curses addressed to people or things.

doctrine—a teaching or principle accepted by religious or philosophic group; dogma.

faith—the unqualified acceptance of and dependence on the completed work of Christ to secure God's mercy.

Hashem—a substitute for the name of God. For traditional Jews the name of God is too holy to be used outside of prayer.

justice—the rightness of God in dealing with his creations, either rewarding, condemning, or judging.

keriah—the cutting or tearing of clothing or a black ribbon prior to funeral.

monotheism—the belief in one God.

omnipotence—the unlimited power of God.

parable—a story in which a moral or spiritual truth is drawn by comparison.

Pentateuch—the first five books of the Hebrew scriptures.

providence—the belief that the events of life are not ruled by chance, but according to God's sovereign plan.

pseudepigrapha—a Greek term meaning "false inscription."

repentance—the act of changing one's inner attitude toward something or someone.

Sheol—the abode of the dead.

sovereignty—supremacy of authority or rule.

theodicy—a vindication of God's goodness and justice in the face of the existence of evil.

Further Reading

BOOKS FOR YOUNG READERS

Coogan, Michael D. *The Old Testament: A Historical and Literary Introduction to Hebrew Scriptures*. New York: Oxford University Press, 2005

Hester, David C. *Interpretation Bible Studies: Job*. Westminster: John Knox, 2005.

Lawson, Steven J. *Holman Old Testament Commentary: Job*. Nashville: Broadman & Holman, 2004.

Mitchell, Stephen. *The Book of Job*. London: Harper Perennial, 1992.

Sutherland, Robert. *Putting God on Trial: The Biblical Book of Job*. Canada: Trafford, 2006.

BOOKS FOR ADULTS

Boadt, Lawrence, ed. *The Book of Job: Why Do the Innocent Suffer?* New York: St. Martin's, 1999.

Eaton , J.H. *Job*. London: T&T Clark International, 2004.

Green, William Henry. *The Book of Job Unfolded*. Arlington Heights, Ill.: Christian Liberty, 1996.

McGee, J. Vernon. *Job: Thru the Bible*. Nashville: Thomas Nelson, 1990.

Wiersbe, Warren W. *Be Patient: Waiting on God in Difficult Times*. Colorado Springs: SP, 1991.

Internet Resources

http://www.bible.org/

The Web site contains a wealth of tools to aid understanding of the Bible, including a relevant introduction to reading the book of Job written by David Malick. The site provides study aids, forums, podcasts by teachers, and a downloadable Bible. Links are also given for additional resources, which serve to further understanding on numerous topics.

http://www.bookofjob.org

The Web site contains summaries from the book entitled *Putting God on Trial: The Biblical Book of Job*, by defense lawyer Robert Sutherland. The text sets up the story of Job as a court case in which God is put on trial.

http://christiananswers.net

This Web site is devoted to providing the answers to contemporary biblical questions. It includes resources for youth and adults.

http://www.cresourcei.org/jobintro.html

Maintained by the nonprofit organization CRI/Voice, this site includes a detailed introduction to the book of Job written by Dennis Bratcher, as well as a variety of research materials.

http://www.greatcom.org/
> This Web site maintained by Global Media Outreach and the Campus Crusade for Christ provides answers to thought-provoking biblical questions.

http://www.jewishvirtuallibrary.org
> This site, maintained by the American-Israeli Cooperative Enterprise, hosts a comprehensive online encyclopedia, including the entire Tanakh.

http://www.studylight.org/
> Considered a "Christ-centered Bible-based internet ministry," the site provides weekly columns, study resources, and online forums.

http://theologytoday.ptsem.edu/
> *Theology Today* is a quarterly ecumenical journal of Christian theology published by the Princeton Theological Seminary. The Web site includes current issues and excerpts from previously published articles.

http://www.theologywebsite.com/
> Community Internet site devoted to providing theological content in a public forum. Theological discourse is presented academically from a traditional, evangelical viewpoint.

Index

Abelman, David, 45
Abraham, 7, 8, *13*, 18, 51, 63
Adam and Eve, 36, 51, 80, 86
Apocrypha, 16
   See also Testament of Job
Aquinas, Thomas, 83–84
Aram, 25
Arthurian legends, 91–92
   See also literature adaptations (of Job)
Ayyub (Job), 18, 55
   See also Job; Qur'an

Balaam, 32
Barakel the Buzite, 73
Bender, Bert, 94
Bible
   and the Apocrypha, 16
   authorship, 15
   See also New Testament; Old Testament
Bible, Hebrew (Tanakh), 17
Bildad (Job's friend), 56–57, 59, 61–73
Book of Job. *See* Job (Old Testament book)
Book of the Dead, 72
Bozrah, 23
Buber, Martin, 41

Calvin, John, 40, 83–84, 87
   and God's refusal to reveal himself, 77
   and suffering, 37–38
Camus, Albert, 92–93
Chumash (Pentateuch), 13, 17
   See also Old Testament
Cooper, Alan, 31, 41–42, 55, 100

Deuteronomy (Old Testament book), 8, *13*, 70
   See also Old Testament
diseases, 46–49, *58*
Documentary Hypothesis, 15
   See also Bible

Eaton, J. H., 21, 44, 49, 59, 72
Egypt, 16–17, 30–31, 32
Elihu, 73–75, 85
Eliphaz (Job's friend), 56–57, 59, 61–73, 75
Esau, 26, 62
Eve and Adam, 36, 51, 80, 86

faith
   and wealth, 6, 7–9
Fohrer, Georg, 14
Frost, Robert, 99

Gill, John, 26
Ginzberg, Louis, 32, *41*, 67
God
   Job's questioning of, 22, 63–65, 76–77, 79

Numbers in **bold italics** refer to captions.

response of, to Job, 79–85
and Satan's wager about Job, 37–42, 45–46, 49, 68
sovereign power of, 18–19, 84, 101, 103
See also Satan
Greek mythology, 97–99
See also literature adaptations (of Job)
Green, William Henry, 22, 35, 37, 38–39, 71, 74, 80
Gregory the Great (Pope), *58*, 99
Guide of the Perplexed (Maimonides), 19–20

ha-Satan. *See* Satan
Hagar, 51
Hesiod, 97–99
Hugo, Victor, *92*

Isaac, 18
Isaiah, 84
Ishmael, 51
Israel, 14

J.B.: A Play in Verse (MacLeish), 94–96
See also literature adaptations (of Job)
Jerome, *79*
Jesus, 9, 36, 38
Jethro, 32
Job
death of, 88
diseases of, 46–49, *58*
early life of, 23
in Egypt, 16–17, 30–31, 32
existence of, 14, 16
family of, 23, 26, 28–29, 44–45, 49, 51–55, 56, 87–88
friends of, 56–57, 59, 61–75, 85–86
generosity of, 6, 8, 29–30, 34, 72, 75
God's response to, 79–85
life of, after suffering, 85–88, 103
in literature, 90–99
meaning of the story of, 99–101

pride of, 6, 34, 84
questions God, 22, 63–65, 76–77, 79
story of, as fable, 19–22
suffering and trials of, 6, 11, 18, 37–49, *58*, 59–62, 103
time period of, 26
wealth of, 6, 23–24, 26–31, 33–34
wife of, 49, 51–55, 56
and wisdom, 30–31
and worms, 48–49
See also Job (Old Testament book); Testament of Job
Job (Old Testament book)
authorship of, 12–14, 16
Elihu's speech, 73
God and Satan, 68
God's punishment of the wicked, 65
God's response to Job, 81, *82*, 83
Job praises God, 45
Job questions God, 63–64, 77, 79
and Job's children, 28, 44
and Job's curses, 59, 93
and Job's diseases, 46–47
Job's friends, 59, 62–63, 65, 66, 67, 69, *70*, 71, 86
and Job's generosity, 72
Job's hope for the future, 69
and Job's pride, 6, 34
and Job's suffering, 40, 43, 44, 46, 60, 61
and Job's wealth, 6, 23–24, 33, 34
and Job's wife, 51
and mourning (keriah), 45
opening line, 23
and Satan, 36, 38, 39
and the theophany, *102*
See also Job; Testament of Job
Jobab, 23
See also Job
"Job's comforter," 56
"Job's post," 97
John XXII (Pope), *50*
Judaism, 17
and rabbinical literature, 30–31

Kassiah (Job's daughter), 88

Index 117

keriah (expression of grief), **44**, 45
Ketuvim (Hebrew Book of Job), 17
Kirsch, Jonathan, 17–18

Lawson, Steven J., 12, 13, 14, 18, 37, 63, 66, 81, 83, 84
legends, Jewish, 8
Legends of the Jews (Ginzberg), 32, **41**, **67**
leviathan, 36, 81–82
  See also Satan
literature adaptations (of Job), 90–99
livestock, 27
  See also wealth
Long, Thomas, 14, 31, 40

MacArthur, John, 89
MacLeish, Archibald, 94–96
Magdalene, F. Rachel, 51–52, 53
Maimonides (Moshe ben Maimon), 19–20, 100
Makos, Jeff, 99
A Masque of Reason (Frost), 99
  See also literature adaptations (of Job)
Melville, Herman, 93–94
Michelangelo, **79**
Moby-Dick (Melville), 93–94
  See also literature adaptations (of Job)
Moralia in Iob, 58
Moses, 13, 15, 17–18, 32, 48, 70–71, **78**, **79**
Murillo, Bartolome Esteban, **10**

Nahmanides (Moshe ben Nahman Gerondi), 20
New Testament, 7, 9, 36

Old Testament, 12, **13**, 23, 51
  Adam and Eve, 36
  and Isaiah's sinfulness, 84
  and Job's friends, 62
  and leprosy, 48
  and obedience to God, 70
  and origin of sin, 86
  and Uz, 24–25
  and viewing God, **78**
  and wealth, 7–8, 9
  See also Job (Old Testament book)
The Only Problem (Spark), 96–97
  See also literature adaptations (of Job)
Ozick, Cynthia, 33, 84, 94

"patience of Job," 97
Pentateuch (Chumash), 13, 17
  See also Old Testament
The Plague (Camus), 93–94
  See also literature adaptations (of Job)
Pope, Marvin, 14
Prometheus, 97–99
  See also literature adaptations (of Job)
pseudepigrapha (Apocrypha), 16

Qur'an, 12, 18, **19**, 54–55

Rahma (Job's wife), 54–55
Rubens, Peter Paul, **57**

Saint Catherine's Monastery, **78**
Sarah, 51
Satan, 14, 18, 35–36, 49, 68, 80, 81
  and Job's wife, 51–52, 53–54
  tests Job's faith, 6, 37–41, 43–44, 45–47
  See also God
Schreiner, Susan E., 11, 40, 83–84, 87, 90, 96, 99
Sefer Iyov (Hebrew Book of Job), 17
Shaitan. *See* Satan
Sheol, 60
Sitidos (Job's wife), 53–54
Solomon (King), 14
Spark, Muriel, 96–97
suicide, 59–60

Talmud, 12, 22
Tanakh (Hebrew Bible), 17
Teitelbaum, Eli, 30
Testament of Job, 16–17
  and Job's friends, 74–75
  Job's life after suffering, 87, 88
  and Job's suffering, 44

118 *Job*

and Job's use of wealth, 29–30
and Satan, 37
and Sitidos (Job's wife), 53–54
and worms, 48–49
See also Job (Old Testament book)
Theogony (Hesiod), 97–99
See also literature adaptations (of Job)
theophany, *102*
Torah, 15, 17

Uz, 22, 23–26, 44
Uz (son of Aram), 25

Uzziah (King), 84

Vulgate, *79*

wealth
and faith, 6, 7–9
of Job, 6, 23–24, 26–31, 33–34
Wiersbe, Warren W., 39, 48, 52, 65, 99–100

Zerah, 23
Zophar (Job's friend), 56–57, 59, 61–73

Illustration Credits

2: Tate, London/Art Resource, NY
10: Scala/Art Resource, NY
13: © 2009 Jupiterimages Corporation
19: Used under license from Shutterstock, Inc.
24: Used under license from Shutterstock, Inc.
27: Used under license from Shutterstock, Inc.
28: Erich Lessing/Art Resource, NY
32: © 2009 Jupiterimages Corporation
36: Used under license from Shutterstock, Inc.
38: Library of Congress
41: Scala/Art Resource, NY
44: Bildarchiv Preussiscer Kulturbesitz/Art Resource, NY
47: Bildarchiv Preussiscer Kulturbesitz/Art Resource, NY
50: The Art Archive / Bibliotheque Universitaire de Medecine, Montpellier / Gianni Dagli Orti
57: Reunion des Musees Nationaux/Art Resource, NY
58: Snark/Art Resource, NY
61: Erich Lessing/Art Resource, NY
64: Doré Bible Illustrations/Creationism.org
67: Image Select/Art Resource, NY
70: Used under license from Shutterstock, Inc.
78: Used under license from Shutterstock, Inc.
79: Used under license from Shutterstock, Inc.
82: Used under license from Shutterstock, Inc.
85: Bildarchiv Preussiscer Kulturbesitz/Art Resource, NY
86: Used under license from Shutterstock, Inc.
92: © 2009 Jupiterimages Corporation
95: Bildarchiv Preussiscer Kulturbesitz/Art Resource, NY
98: Used under license from Shutterstock, Inc.
102: Cameraphoto/Art Resource, NY

Cover photo: Erich Lessing / Art Resource, NY

CAMERON CHRISTINE DAVIS received her BA in English-Creative Writing from Western Michigan University and her MA in English at the University of Florida, where she specialized in cultural studies. She has written biographies for various publications and is currently working on a book of poems and short stories with her husband. She teaches tenth grade English in Texas, where she lives with her husband and Labrador retriever, Lola.